MW01229338

THE WAYFINDER

Copyright © 2024 by Daniel Slack-Smith

All rights reserved.

No portion of this book may be reproduced in any form without written
permission from the publisher or author except as permitted by U.S.
copyright law.

ISBN (hardcover): 979-8-9900404-1-0
ISBN (e-book): 979-8-9900404-0-3

Library of Congress Control Number: 2024903395

Book design by Albatross Book Co.

Published by Naremburn in San Diego, California, USA

Inquiries: info@naremburn.com

THE WAYFINDER

The Life of the Late Sheikh Zayed bin Sultan Al Nahyan
Founding President of the United Arab Emirates

DANIEL SLACK-SMITH

NAREMBURN

San Diego | California

Contents

PROLOGUE

On December 2, 1971, the fifty-three-year-old Ruler of Abu Dhabi, Sheikh Zayed bin Sultan Al Nahyan, rose from his chair at Union House, Dubai, and walked the short distance to the modest flagpole outside. Photographers perched on the roof of the low-slung building eagerly snapped away at the historic scene unfolding below them. Moments earlier, Abu Dhabi and five of its neighboring states had formed an unlikely political union that most regional analysts expected to fail. While the ink was still drying on the founding documents inside, the national flag of that new country, the United Arab Emirates, would now be raised for the first time on what was then still the shoreline of the Gulf.

Sheikh Zayed, who had just been selected by his fellow Rulers to serve as the UAE's founding President, looked confident as he strode out into the winter sunlight for the raising of the flag, but history was not on his side. After all, the six emirates joining forces that day (Ras Al

Khaimah would join two months later) had not always been on the same page. Even Abu Dhabi and Dubai, the two largest partners at the center of the union, had been engaged in violent border clashes with one another just over two decades earlier.

However, with the British Government withdrawing its forces from the region after 150 years, and with no powerful ally to protect them, the choice for the fractious emirates in 1971 was as simple as it was grave: They could fight amongst themselves, or they could survive together.

Of course, this wasn't a new idea to Sheikh Zayed. It was one of the first things that he had ever learned as a child.

— ONE —
Sheikh Zayed Was Born

Sheikh Zayed is born into Abu Dhabi's ruling Al Nahyan family in 1918. Three Abu Dhabi Rulers – including his father and two of his uncles – are murdered before he turns ten. When Sheikh Zayed's eldest brother becomes Ruler of Abu Dhabi in 1928, his mother extracts a pledge from her sons that they will never use violence against each other.

Sheikh Zayed was born in Abu Dhabi on May 6, 1918. That's the nearest thing there is to a consensus on the matter. In reality, the only part of that sentence that historians know for sure is the first four words: Sheikh Zayed was born. Nobody can prove exactly where or when it happened, because no record of his birth has ever been found. Some people are adamant that he was born in Al Ain, but there is no evidence for that either. An obscure travel document issued to Sheikh Zayed by a foreign government in the 1950s states that he was born in 1915, but doesn't say where, while other sources suggest that he was actually born in 1916. It is hard to imagine now, but it appears that the life of one of the most transformative historical figures of the twentieth century may well have begun without a single note being taken.

What we do know is that Sheikh Zayed was the youngest of four brothers, that he had a sister named Mariam, and that his early childhood was rocked by an intense period of tribal political violence involving his father and at least two of his uncles. There's no way to sugarcoat it: Abu Dhabi in the 1920s was a dangerous place, and a violent power struggle was looming within the ruling Al Nahyan family.

In 1922, when Sheikh Zayed was around four years of age, his father – Sheikh Sultan – allegedly killed his own brother, Sheikh Hamdan, to become the Ruler of Abu Dhabi and the new leader of the Bani Yas tribal confederation. The Bani Yas was a powerful alliance of tribes, sub-tribes and families that inhabited the vast territory of Abu Dhabi. The Ruler of Abu Dhabi, and by extension, the leader of the Bani Yas, was traditionally selected from among the members of the Al Nahyan family, which headed the *Al Bu Falah* section of the alliance. Sheikh Sultan formally notified the British Government of his brother's demise and his own accession as the Ruler of Abu Dhabi in a short letter to the local Residency Agent in August 1922, noting fatalistically that "a thing that has to happen can not be escaped."

Notifying the British Government of such a change was more than a mere courtesy at the time. For the previous hundred years, diplomatic relations between the British Government and the Trucial States – including Abu Dhabi – had been governed by a series of treaties (or "truces," hence the name, Trucial States), initially focused on securing freedom of navigation for British ships along the so-called 'Pirate Coast,' an infamous stretch of water where vessels had historically been raided by seafaring tribes, but eventually including a range of other provisions that effectively made these Arab Sheikhdoms informal protectorates of the British Empire.

At the time, advancing UK interests in the Gulf was primarily the responsibility of the British Government of India, which was represented in the area by a high-ranking official known as the Political Resident (also known as the British Resident), based in the Persian city of Bushire until 1946. Even though the stated policy in relation to the Trucial States was one of non-intervention, British officials were not averse to firing off a terse letter, or even naval artillery, if they felt that their interests were being threatened in any way. Another common form of British 'non-intervention' in the affairs of the Trucial States involved the deployment of armed naval ships close to the shore in a threatening practice known as gunboat diplomacy.

The three main treaties between the UK Government and the Trucial States make for dull reading, but they are integral to understanding the politics of the Gulf during this period. The first agreement, the General Treaty for the Cessation of Plunder and Piracy by Land and Sea of 1820, outlawed piracy against British ships and slave trading along the Gulf coast. The second agreement, the Perpetual Maritime Truce of 1853, banned all hostilities at sea, including between the local tribes, and empowered the British navy to keep the peace in the waters of the Gulf. Finally, the Exclusive Agreements of 1892 effectively outsourced the foreign and trade policies of the Trucial States to the British Government in exchange for British protection, including preventing the Rulers of the Trucial States from entering into agreements or even corresponding with any other foreign power. This last one would end up having major political consequences when the search for oil on the Arabian Peninsula began to ramp up in the middle of the twentieth century.

When a new Ruler came to power in one of the Trucial States, one of his first official duties was to notify the British Government of his intention to abide by these existing treaties. It was not essential that he had actually read them. We know this because in the exchange of diplomatic letters that occurred after Sheikh Zayed's father, Sheikh Sultan, took over as Ruler of Abu Dhabi in 1922, and after he had solemnly sworn to honor these agreements, it was eventually revealed that after a thorough search of the late Ruler's residence, nobody in Abu Dhabi could find the 'Book of Treaties,' and the British Government agreed to send out a replacement copy. However, this new edition would not be in Sheikh Sultan's possession for long, because four years into his tenure as Ruler, he was murdered by another of his brothers – Sheikh Saqr – who would rule Abu Dhabi for just two years before he too was killed, in 1928.

Due to his age at the time of these events, it is often assumed that Sheikh Zayed must have had no memories of his father, but reflecting on his childhood in 1974, he appears to have vividly recalled going on family hunting trips as a boy, telling the author Claud Morris: "With my father I would cross by water on a dhow to the other side, from Abu Dhabi. We had about thirty with us . . . We started every morning at 4:00 a.m. when the light was coming. If the shooting or falconry was good we returned earlier, for we had to carry our own game." It isn't conclusive, but the details of this story lend some credence to the theory that Sheikh Zayed might have been born a few years earlier than 1918 (which would have made him only eight by the time his father died in 1926).

The young Sheikh Zayed was largely sheltered from the political violence of the 1920s, but he was undoubtedly aware of the fear and loss that swirled around him as a child. Although versions of this story differ on the details, it is generally believed that shortly before Sheikh Zayed's father was murdered in 1926, he instructed his eldest son, Sheikh Shakhbut, to urgently get his mother and youngest brother out of Abu Dhabi, where he feared for their safety, and to transfer them to the inland area of Buraimi, which included the village of Al Ain. It was a dangerous journey, but one that may well have saved the life of the future UAE founder. Sheikh Zayed would never see his father again, but the lessons of those violent and unproductive years in Abu Dhabi would remain with him for life.

Shortly after his uncle's death in 1928, Sheikh Zayed's eldest brother, Sheikh Shakhbut, was selected to become the new Ruler of Abu Dhabi at around twenty-five years of age. Based on the events of the previous six years, he must have doubted that he would live to see thirty. As it turned out, Sheikh Shakhbut would end up living comfortably into his eighties, passing away peacefully in 1989. It wasn't all smooth sailing, including between him and his brothers, but the knives would never come out in the same way again.

The key to ending the cycle of violence came in the diminutive form of the new Ruler's mother, Sheikha Salama bint Butti. Known colloquially as *Umm Al Shiyukh* (the Mother of the Sheikhs), Sheikha Salama was a lot more than that. Often described as a force of nature, she would become one of the most consequential figures in the history of Abu Dhabi. Born in a small village called Muzaira, near the Liwa oasis in the western part of Abu Dhabi territory, Sheikha Salama was born into the prominent *Qubaisat* section of the Bani Yas. Having grown up in the desert, she was an expert in the use of traditional, plant-based medicine, and years before the discovery of oil in Abu Dhabi, she famously gave Sheikh Zayed a small bottle of crude oil that she had procured so that he would know what it looked like if he saw it.

In 1928, after three assassinations in six years, and with her eldest son now squarely in the line of fire, Sheikha Salama took matters into her own hands and extracted a pledge from her sons that they would stand together and never use violence against one another. It turned out to be the circuit breaker that the Al Nahyan family needed, and Sheikh Zayed and his brothers would remain devoted to their mother and faithful to the pledge that they had made to her for the rest of their lives.

TWO

The Pride of Al Ain

Sheikh Zayed takes refuge in the oasis village of Al Ain around the time of his father's death in 1926. Growing up in Al Ain exposes him to the traditional lifestyle of the Bedouin from an early age and equips him with a natural fluency in the tribal politics of the area.

The city of Al Ain (which means "the spring" in Arabic) lies one hundred miles inland from the city of Abu Dhabi. Once a multi-day journey by camel, getting there now takes around ninety minutes by car. It's a dramatic improvement, but evidently still not quick enough for some motorists on the E22 highway, who seem determined to do it in half that time. With a population of just under eight hundred thousand people, comparable in size to Liverpool in England or Seattle in the United States, Al Ain is a large city in global terms, but up close it feels more like a sprawling town. Large parts of it didn't get electricity until 1972.

When Sheikh Zayed took shelter near there as a child in the 1920s, Al Ain was one of nine sandy villages connected to the Buraimi Oasis complex, near the present-day border with Oman. At the time, the settlement of Al Ain consisted of a functioning oasis connected to an ingenious but crumbling irrigation system, a number of aging forts, some mud brick houses and palm frond huts, and an outdoor market that serviced the local population and Bedouin travelers that would emerge from the nearby Empty Quarter. British officials in the region, focused primarily on policing the waters of the Gulf, took very little interest in the affairs of the inland towns, and the tribes of the interior were mostly left to their own devices.

Historical descriptions of the hinterland around this time make it sound like an Arabian version of the Old West. Cars were non-existent. Snake and scorpion bites were common. The theft of camels by armed desert raiders was a regular occurrence, often followed by violent counter-raids. Men carried rifles and wore *khanjars* (traditional daggers) on their waists. Powerful Sheikhs assembled groups of retainers or hired guns to protect them. Some desert outlaws became legendary, their bloody deeds known throughout the region. It is hard to comprehend that this was where Sheikh Zayed was sent as a child for his own safety, but it was apparently less dangerous than keeping him on the coast.

Although it would be the subject of an armed dispute in the 1950s, it was generally understood that six of the villages around the Buraimi Oasis (Al Ain, Hili, Jimi, Mutaredh, Muwaiji and Qattara) were under the jurisdiction of the Ruler of Abu Dhabi, while the other three (Hamasa, Buraimi and Saara) were under the jurisdiction of the Sultan of Muscat and Oman. These historical ties would have lasting geopolitical implications. When the negotiation of oil concessions in the 1930s made it necessary to establish borders between the Trucial States, and with their neighbors in Oman and Saudi Arabia, the traditional allegiances of the people on the ground became the most important factor for determining where those lines would be drawn.

Inland oases such as Al Ain were integral to the traditional pattern of life of the Bani Yas people. Although they are often described as a nomadic or Bedouin tribe, the truth is that by the end of the nineteenth century, most members of the Bani Yas were not nomads at all. Rather than roaming the deserts, they lived a mobile but semi-settled existence, and their seasonal movements were highly predictable. Each year, at the beginning of the pearling season (roughly April to October), most men would find work on one of the pearling boats setting sail from Abu Dhabi, or in the provision of other services to the pearling fleet. Outside of the pearling season, and after the pearling industry declined across the board in the 1930s, many of these same men could be found farming or growing dates at one of the inland oases.

These weren't the only jobs available. Some fished, raised livestock or provided security as armed retainers. Others maintained a lucrative side hustle transporting people through the desert by camel. Certain sections of the Bani Yas became known for specializing in particular economic activities, but in this early iteration of a gig economy, most people did more than one thing for a living.

In her 1982 book, *From Trucial States to United Arab Emirates*, Frauke Heard-Bey described this phenomenon with an economic archetype dubbed "the versatile tribesman":

"He is to be found throughout the area and throughout the ages. He spends the winter with his livestock in the desert and comes to the coast to fish in the summer in order to supplement his own and his animals' diet. He plants or harvests his dates and takes part in the pearling, or he sows and harvests his millet high up in the mountains and spends the hot months of the summer fishing at the coast, or he leads a caravan or steers a ship and then returns to engage in some quite different activity. In short, there have been at all times in this area not a few tribesmen, every one of whom knew all there was to know about camel-breeding, pearling, farming, fishing or sailmaking."

It is often noted that members of the Bani Yas would leave Abu Dhabi and take refuge in Al Ain during the hottest months of the year. Those that could afford it owned homes and date gardens there for precisely this purpose. In fact, Sheikh Zayed's grandfather had built a fortified "royal summer residence" (Al Jahili Fort) in Al Ain in the late 1800s, where he and his family could escape the heat of the coast. It sounds luxurious, but the reality is that even Al Ain in the summer is not particularly comfortable. In fact, it is generally hotter there than it is in Abu Dhabi, just less humid.

Al Ain would have a formative influence on the young Sheikh Zayed, just as he would later have a transformative impact on it. Although reliable information on precisely where Sheikh Zayed was, and what he was doing, during the first twenty-five years of his life is surprisingly hard to come by (including how much time he spent in Abu Dhabi during this period, with at least one account suggesting that he may even have moved back there for a while with his mother), it is generally believed that he spent the majority of his childhood and adolescence in Al Ain. The city of Al Ain certainly claims him as one of their own to this day.

According to one depiction of these early years, although his formal education consisted mainly of studying the Quran, Sheikh Zayed's upbringing in Al Ain also included spending a lot of time in the *majlis* of his maternal grandfather, where the future Ruler "saw at first hand the tribal issues and concerns which he had largely experienced second hand in Abu Dhabi." When and how he had experienced these things in Abu Dhabi is not explained. In any case, Sheikh Zayed's easy fluency in the politics and culture of the area, which he would later use to great effect as the Ruler's Representative in the Eastern Region of Abu Dhabi, is widely believed to stem from the years that he spent in and around the desert, mountains and oases in his youth.

Growing up on the edge of the Empty Quarter also exposed Sheikh Zayed to the traditional customs and self-sufficient lifestyle of the local Bedouin tribes, which he took to from an early age. "I loved riding and hunting. These were my passions," Sheikh Zayed would recall when reflecting on his own childhood many years later.

According to the late Sayed Abdullah bin Ghanom, who served as the young Sheikh Zayed's teacher and religious instructor throughout this period: "The boy would go up on Jebel Hafeet, on the boundary between Abu Dhabi and Oman. He would shoot and hunt gazelle with amazing persistence. He was the most fearless boy I had ever met. He didn't mind the weather. It could be hot beyond bearing or very cold. His father told me always to watch him. Yet he went his own way with his falcons and his guns. You could be in camp in a group and suddenly look around, and Zayed had gone like the wind."

Sheikh Zayed's lifelong interest in camels, hunting, falconry, Bedouin life and the ancient customs of the desert tribes, can be traced directly to the traditional environment in which he grew up. Perhaps ironically, his intimate knowledge of the area would also bring him into direct contact with the agents who were determined to upend that traditional lifestyle forever.

In one of the first signs of the changes that were looming on the horizon, in the late 1930s, when Sheikh Zayed was around the age of twenty, he was hand-picked by his brother, Sheikh Shakhbut, to act as a desert wayfinder for some of the first British geologists to arrive in Abu Dhabi in search of oil and water beneath the sand.

— THREE —
Sheikh Zayed at Thirty

Sheikh Zayed is appointed Ruler's Representative in the Eastern Region of Abu Dhabi in 1946. He initiates a major restoration and expansion of the local water supply and establishes a more equitable system for the distribution of this precious resource. In 1948, he becomes a father at the age of thirty with the birth of his first son, Khalifa.

It is a universal law of politics that taking away a benefit that people have grown accustomed to polls badly. Unfortunately for Sheikh Zayed's brother, Sheikh Shakhbut, that's precisely what he had to do shortly after coming to power as the new Ruler of Abu Dhabi and leader of the Bani Yas in 1928. The development of the cultured pearl in Japan, combined with the advent of the Great Depression, led to the near-total collapse of the local pearling industry – which had sustained the Abu Dhabi economy for generations – within a few devastating years.

As his tax revenues plummeted, the new Ruler was unable to maintain the generous subsidies that had previously flowed into the hands of local tribal leaders since the time of his grandfather, and which had become integral to maintaining their support. This fiscal contraction, coming on the heels of almost a decade of political instability, created a situation in which the authority of the ruling Al Nahyan family was becoming increasingly fragile in the inland areas of Abu Dhabi territory, including around Al Ain.

This was a politically dangerous development. As Rosemarie Said Zahlan explained in her 1978 book, *The Origins of the United Arab Emirates: A Political and Social History of the Trucial States:* "The foremost measure of a coastal ruler's strength and prestige was his ability to command the tribes of the interior; his rise or decline in coastal politics could usually be measured by his ability to enforce his authority over the tribal chieftains in the area he claimed as his territory."

This may have had as much to do with geography as it did with politics. With water to one side of them, and a treaty with the British Government prohibiting attacks by sea, the most immediate threat to a coastal Ruler's position was the possibility of one inland tribe or another abruptly shifting its loyalties to a rival power. The Bedouin tribes understood this power dynamic too, of course, and by the time Sheikh Zayed was coming of age in Al Ain in the mid-1930s, he would have been acutely aware that his family's standing in the area was potentially in decline. What nobody knew was that he would be the one to reverse the trend.

In 1946, Sheikh Shakhbut appointed his youngest brother, the twenty-eight-year-old Sheikh Zayed, to be his official representative or *wali* in the Eastern Region of Abu Dhabi (an area that was often simply referred to at the time as "Buraimi"), which encompassed Al Ain. In the same year, Sheikh Shakhbut appointed the second-eldest of the four brothers, Sheikh Hazza, to serve as his equivalent representative in the Western Region, which included Liwa. The third-eldest of the brothers, Sheikh Khalid, remained in Abu Dhabi town, where he continued to serve as an advisor to the Ruler.

Sheikh Zayed set up his official residence in Qasr Al Muwaiji, adjacent to the Muwaiji oasis, converting the fort's northwest tower into a family home where he lived with his first wife, the late Sheikha Hessa bint Mohammed bin Khalifa Al Nahyan. It was Sheikha Hessa's grandfather, and Al Nahyan family powerbroker, Sheikh Khalifa bin Zayed, who is believed to have originally built Qasr Al Muwaiji between 1905 and 1909. It still stands today and is now a museum.

As the Ruler's Representative, Sheikh Zayed was effectively the local governor of the area. He established his *diwan* (i.e. royal court) in the interior courtyard of Qasr Al Muwaiji, and the palace became a frequent gathering place for the local community during the years in which he held court there. Echoing his grandfather, Zayed the Great, who was photographed doing the same thing at Qasr Al Hosn in Abu Dhabi in 1904, Sheikh Zayed often held his own *majlis* against the exterior wall of Qasr Al Muwaiji, or under a tree outside. It was here that he would receive visitors, exchange news with them, and seek to address their concerns. Visiting Bedouin tribesmen, some of whom were not even permanent subjects of Abu Dhabi, would occasionally ask Sheikh Zayed to adjudicate disputes between them, usually with a small audience of locals listening in.

In his memoir, Edward Henderson (who worked in Abu Dhabi in various capacities over the course of his career, originally as a British oil company representative) described meeting a thirty-year-old Sheikh Zayed for the first time at Qasr Al Muwaiji in November 1948:

"Two days later we called on Shaikh Zayed at Al-Muwaiqi [Muwaiji] fort. This was a rather forbidding square fortress with crenellated corner towers. To exclude the heat, the rooms inside were necessarily rather dark and had no furniture but the colorful rugs and cushions on the floor. Shaikh Zayed was then perhaps 30 years old. He was handsome with humorous and intelligent eyes, of fine presence and bearing, simply dressed, like his cousin Muhammad [bin Khalifah], and clearly a man of action and resolution. Although he was young and had only been formally in charge of the Abu Dhabi sector of the oasis and its surrounding deserts for some two years, he was experienced in the politics of the region and was already by far the most prominent personality in the area. He had a sure touch with the bedouin in both the Abu Dhabi and Muscat areas."

Sheikh Zayed's signature project as the Ruler's Representative in the Eastern Region of Abu Dhabi was the restoration and expansion of the local *aflaj* network (a traditional system of underground tunnels and surface-level irrigation channels that supplied water to the area), which at that time was arguably the most important piece of critical infrastructure in the emirate. Sheikh Zayed initially ordered and funded the repair of large sections of the existing *aflaj* network in order to restore the flow of water to something approaching its earlier capacity, including working on parts of the project himself. He then commissioned the construction of a new, mile-long, underground *falaj* (singular for *aflaj*), known as Al Saruj, that would take around twenty years to complete but would dramatically increase the supply of water to Al Ain and its surrounding villages.

While this new *falaj* was under construction, Sheikh Zayed took on the unfair system that had developed around the ownership and sale of water rights, and which had left some local residents with no access to water at all. When some of those who benefited the most from the existing arrangements initially refused to relinquish any of their rights, Sheikh Zayed reportedly outmaneuvered them by announcing that when the new *falaj* was completed, they would be excluded from accessing it. The tactic worked, and by the time the new *falaj* came online, a more equitable system had been established for the distribution of the area's scarce water resources.

Two years into his tenure as the Ruler's Representative, Sheikh Zayed also became a father with the birth of his first son, Sheikh Khalifa bin Zayed Al Nahyan, who would eventually succeed him as the Ruler of Abu Dhabi and President of the UAE. Sheikh Khalifa was born while Sheikh Zayed was in Abu Dhabi on government business, so a lone messenger rode by camel from Al Ain to the coast in a day – a journey that normally took three days – to bring him the good news as soon as possible. Just two months after this epic ride, the need to repeat it would be consigned to history when British oil executives installed a radio room at Al Ain's Jahili Fort that could communicate instantaneously with the corresponding unit at Qasr Al Hosn.

Like Edward Henderson before him, it was at Qasr Al Muwaiji that the famed British explorer Wilfred Thesiger also met Sheikh Zayed for the first time in 1948. Thesiger described his initial encounter with the young Ruler's Representative in a well-worn passage from his epic book, *Arabian Sands*:

"I greeted them and exchanged the news with Zayid. He was a powerfully built man of about thirty with a brown beard. He had a strong, intelligent face, with steady, observant eyes, and his manner was quiet but masterful. He was dressed, very simply, in a beige-coloured shirt of Omani cloth, and a waistcoat which he wore unbuttoned. He was distinguished from his companions by his black head-rope, and the way in which he wore his head-cloth, falling about his shoulders instead of twisted round his head in the local manner. He wore a dagger and cartridge-belt; his rifle lay on the sand beside him.

I had been looking forward to meeting him, for he had a great reputation among the Bedu. They liked him for his easy informal ways and his friendliness, and they respected his force of character, his shrewdness, and his physical strength. They said admiringly, 'Zayid is a Bedu. He knows about camels, can ride like one of us, can shoot, and knows how to fight.'"

Thesiger established a strong rapport with Sheikh Zayed during the month that he spent in Al Ain, enjoying his hospitality, joining him on a hunting trip, and even borrowing his most prized camel, *Ghazala*, to ride to Sharjah at the end of his stay. However, he was never one to pull his punches, and in his writings and public statements, Thesiger openly expressed his sorrow at the Arabian people's inexorable march into modernity and their inevitable abandonment of their traditional way of life, asserting somewhat sweepingly that, "the Arabs are a race which produces its best only under conditions of extreme hardship and deteriorates progressively as living conditions become easier."

While people often cite Thesiger's glowing first impressions of the thirty-year-old Sheikh Zayed, less attention is paid to what he wrote in the preface to *Arabian Sands* in 1984, where he described modern Abu Dhabi as "an Arabian nightmare, the final disillusionment," and pointedly dedicated his epic book to a "vanished past" and "a once magnificent people." It was a blunt assessment, and one that appeared to place little value on modern amenities such as houses, schools and hospitals, which had dramatically improved the life prospects of the local population in the intervening period. One can only imagine what Thesiger would have made of the air-conditioned shopping mall that is now located across the street from the very spot where he first drank *gahwa* (Arabic coffee) on the ground with a young Sheikh Zayed.

However, there is no evidence that Sheikh Zayed took any offense to this. On the contrary, he appears to have possessed an innate tolerance for views and opinions that differed from his own. In fact, Thesiger would return to Abu Dhabi in 1990 for a photo exhibition, hosted under the patronage of Sheikh Zayed himself. When *Arabian Sands* was reprinted again in 1991, it was the author who felt compelled to bring up his earlier comments, writing in a new preface that he now found himself "reconciled to the inevitable changes which have occurred in the Arabia of today," and going on to describe Abu Dhabi as "an impressive modern city, made pleasant in this barren land by avenues of trees and green lawns."

The most interesting thing about these events is not what Thesiger wrote in 1984 versus what he wrote in 1991.

The man crossed the Empty Quarter twice and was entitled to his opinions. What is more revealing is that Sheikh Zayed never seemed to hold a grudge, in this case with an eccentric British explorer that he met when he was thirty years old, but also in other situations when the offense was potentially greater and the stakes were considerably higher. It would not be long into his tenure as the Ruler's Representative before this capacity would be tested.

FOUR

The Buraimi Dispute

The Kingdom of Saudi Arabia makes a controversial claim for a portion of Abu Dhabi territory, triggering the six-year Buraimi Dispute. Simmering tensions between the Ruler of Abu Dhabi and his brothers prompt a leadership crisis. After arbitration to resolve the Buraimi Dispute fails, the British-led Trucial Oman Levies retake the area by force.

———————

In October 1949, three years after Sheikh Zayed's appointment as the Ruler's Representative in the Eastern Region of Abu Dhabi, the Kingdom of Saudi Arabia made an audacious claim for a large area of land that stretched across parts of Abu Dhabi and Oman. The Abu Dhabi portion of the disputed territory included areas around the Buraimi oasis complex that were under the local supervision of

Sheikh Zayed. This marked the beginning of the six-year diplomatic saga known as the Buraimi Dispute.

There is little doubt that the Buraimi Dispute was largely precipitated by the search for oil on the Arabian Peninsula and the need to establish borders where none had previously existed. In fact, the Saudi claim that triggered the dispute reportedly occurred after an oil exploration party from the US oil company, Aramco, accompanied by Saudi guards, entered Abu Dhabi territory, where it was confronted by Patrick Stobart, the British Political Officer in the Trucial States, who was accompanied by his own armed guards. The altercation in the desert led to a heated diplomatic standoff, and an agreement was hastily struck in 1950 to cease all oil exploration activity in the area until these territorial issues could be resolved.

In 1951, with the situation on the border no closer to being resolved, Sheikh Zayed was struck down with measles and traveled to Dubai to receive treatment at the newly-established Al Maktoum Hospital. The only silver lining was that a meeting at his hospital bedside between the Rulers of Abu Dhabi and Dubai led to an uneasy truce in the volatile boundary dispute that had waxed and waned between the two Sheikhdoms and their proxies for years. It was one less thing to worry about at an ominous time.

Back in Buraimi, things were just getting started. In September 1952, after almost two years of stalled negotiations, Turki bin Abdullah al Otaishan, the Emir of Ras Tanura in the eastern part of Saudi Arabia, abruptly led a convoy of vehicles into the Omani village of Hamasa and claimed Saudi Arabian sovereignty over the surrounding area. From his foothold in Hamasa, al Otaishan began immediately reaching out to the nearby villages and tribes, including some who had traditionally been loyal to the Ruler of Abu Dhabi, offering cash and other inducements to encourage them to pledge their allegiance to the Kingdom of Saudi Arabia. The majority of Abu Dhabi subjects resisted these overtures, but some did not, with the lure of such largesse in an era of extreme deprivation proving too tempting to refuse.

In response to the Saudi incursion, the British Government deployed a military force including one hundred members of the Trucial Oman Levies to blockade the village of Hamasa, requiring supplies to be dropped in by air. Created in 1951, the Trucial Oman Levies (which later became the Trucial Oman Scouts) were a local military force established by the British Government for the purposes of maintaining law and order outside of the major towns of the Trucial States. Two years into the blockade, the parties to the Buraimi Dispute – Britain on behalf of both Abu Dhabi and Oman on one side, and Saudi Arabia on the other – agreed to attempt to settle the dispute via arbitration in Geneva at the beginning of 1955.

Even if he had wanted to, Sheikh Zayed was in no position to compete in a bidding war with Saudi Arabia for the hearts and minds of local residents. In fact, British officials were highly concerned about Sheikh Zayed's financial situation around this time, noting in private correspondence that the costs of fulfilling his responsibilities in Al Ain – including upgrading the local *aflaj* system and providing men to assist in the ongoing blockade of Hamasa – had left him heavily in debt to members of his family and others. They calculated that the limited allowance that Sheikh Zayed received from his brother in Abu Dhabi, as well as the taxes he earned locally from date farming and irrigation levies (most of which was reinvested in the *aflaj* project), did not come close to covering his monthly expenses. It was even rumored at one point that he had "pawned his wife's jewels" to help meet the shortfall.

The Ruler of Abu Dhabi, Sheikh Shakhbut, appears to have been strangely indifferent to this situation, despite repeated entreaties from his brothers and British officials for him to show greater generosity to the people around Buraimi, whose loyalty was now being tested. Sheikh Shakhbut consistently brushed off these warnings, demonstrating a breathtaking reluctance to part with money even when it was in his own interests to do so. It may have been too late to change his ways in any case, with one British official lamenting that, "Unfortunately even if it is true that he is now more generous with visiting *bedu* than he was, and I very much doubt it, his reputation for parsimony is such that few of them will now trouble to make the journey to Abu Dhabi to put him to the test."

In the records from this period, Sheikh Shakhbut comes across as a complex but ultimately sympathetic character, whose outlook had been indelibly shaped by his own austere upbringing, with Sheikh Zayed once saying of his older brother that he never saw the value of anything new. In the sanctuary of his private *majlis* and library, he would spend hours listening to the BBC World Service on an old Grundig radio, and reading the news with the benefit of a utilitarian pair of black-rimmed glasses. Despite his legendary aversion to extravagance, he also inexplicably drove around Abu Dhabi – and occasionally into the nearby sand dunes – in a bright yellow convertible Cadillac with fins. In his book, *This Strange Eventful History*, the late Edward Henderson observed that "Sheikh Shakhbut would hold forth on any subject and had the shrewdest questions to ask, whether about flying saucers or the population of Bristol, the rainfall in Scotland or the politics of the Middle East."

Due to the manner in which his reign ultimately came to an end, the positive impact that Sheikh Shakhbut had on the emirate over his almost four decades in power is often overlooked. Among other things, he brought stable leadership to Abu Dhabi after almost a decade of turmoil when he became Ruler in 1928, including steering the emirate through the turbulence associated with the collapse of the pearling industry and the Great Depression. Prior to the discovery of oil, he was reportedly the first Trucial State Ruler to recognize the need to clarify his boundaries with his neighbors and the first to invite foreign geologists to explore his land, ostensibly for water but eventually also in the hopes of finding oil. He consistently refused to be pushed around in his interactions with British officials, even when lopsided treaty obligations and power dynamics gave him little room to maneuver, including in negotiations over oil concessions. For example, when the British-owned Petroleum Development Trucial Coast Ltd. challenged Sheikh Shakhbut's right to award an offshore concession to an American company in 1950, he took the issue all the way to international arbitration in Paris, where the Abu Dhabi position was upheld.

However, Sheikh Shakhbut's iron grip on the purse strings would lead to a heated dispute within his own family in early 1954. It all started when he discovered that his brothers had been receiving cash payments as well as supplies of petrol and kerosene from the Anglo Iranian Oil Company, rather than through him. Never mind that these payments were consistent with the terms of the concession agreement that he had signed with the company fifteen years earlier. Furious at this perceived betrayal, Sheikh Shakhbut took it upon himself to deduct the amount of these payments from the next round of allowances that he paid to his brothers, even though their finances were already stretched to the limit.

Sheikh Hazza, the second-eldest of the four, drew the short straw and was nominated to take up the issue on behalf of the three younger brothers. He met with Sheikh Shakhbut at Qasr Al Hosn and calmly objected to the reductions that had been made to their allowances. Not only were the direct payments that he and his brothers had been receiving from the oil company spelled out in the concession agreement, but in the midst of the Buraimi dispute, it was a terrible time for the Ruler's representatives to be forced to tighten their belts. Sheikh Shakhbut's mother, Sheikha Salama, also weighed in on the side of her three youngest sons.

Sheikh Shakhbut, however, was unmoved, and as often happens with family arguments, a much wider array of historical resentments was suddenly on the table. Sheikh Shakhbut angrily defended his decision to dock his brothers' allowances. He blasted them for dealing with the oil company behind his back, and for bringing British officials into the middle of a family disagreement. He also complained bitterly about Sheikh Zayed liaising directly with the British Government in relation to the Buraimi dispute, despite the fact that he was the Ruler's designated representative in the area.

Pushed to his breaking point, an exasperated Sheikh Hazza fired back with a litany of complaints, mostly in relation to Sheikh Shakhbut's treatment of their youngest brother. There was the time that Sheikh Zayed had sent a truck all the way from Al Ain to Abu Dhabi to collect some petrol that he needed, but Sheikh Shakhbut had churlishly sent the truck back empty. There was the fact that Sheikh Shakhbut repeatedly refused Sheikh Zayed's requests for loans and criticized his handling of the Buraimi dispute, while refusing to visit the area to examine the situation for himself. There was also the time three years earlier when

Sheikh Shakhbut had angrily kicked Sheikh Hazza and Sheikh Khalid out of Qasr Al Hosn for bringing up the subject of allowances.

It is unclear what Sheikh Hazza was hoping to achieve with this diatribe, but the response that he got was unexpected. Rather than continuing the argument, Sheikh Shakhbut responded to this laundry list of grievances by offering to resign as Ruler and transfer power to his brothers on the spot. After initially writing this off as just something said in the heat of the moment, Sheikh Hazza quickly realized that his brother was serious. Unwilling to reconsider his position, Sheikh Shakhbut instructed Sheikh Hazza to summon Sheikh Zayed from Al Ain to Abu Dhabi immediately, in order to work out the arrangements for his abdication in consultation with their mother.

When he left the room, a stunned Sheikh Hazza reached out to his brothers to bring them up to speed, and Sheikh Zayed made plans to travel to Abu Dhabi in the coming days. According to one British official who spoke to him about it, before breathlessly relaying the conversation to his colleagues: "Sheikh Zaid said quite simply that he was glad at what had happened. For several years past his work in Buraimi had consisted as to two thirds dealing with Sheikh Shakhbut and as to one third in running the oasis and Shaikh Shakhbut had never been able to see any problem except in the light of his consuming jealousy. The first task of the brothers would be to undo some of the damage that Shaikh Shakhbut's cavalier treatment of them had caused among the tribes."

However, it was a task that would have to wait. When the long-awaited family conclave finally took place at Qasr Al Hosn a few weeks later, it was decided that Sheikh Shakhbut would remain in power after all, with the chastened Ruler making some limited concessions to mollify his brothers and preserve the status quo.

Despite having had their own rocky relationship with Sheikh Shakhbut, British officials were relatively content with the outcome of the abdication crisis. However, their reasoning is revealing, with one senior British official in the Gulf at the time writing that: "Whoever rules in Abu Dhabi it is, I think, essential that Zaid remains in Buraimi, where his presence has been of inestimable value to us. He alone has been able to bolster up the loyal tribes in the Buraimi area in their stand against Saudi encroachment and he must be allowed to continue his excellent work undisturbed by financial worries or family squabbles." It was a pragmatic position, but it provided no guarantee that the British Government would remain on the sidelines if the leadership question ever came up again.

With the matter decided for now, Sheikh Zayed returned to Al Ain to continue serving as his brother's representative, but in private he seemed resigned to the fact that it was only a matter of time before the same issues would resurface. According to one British official writing just weeks after the 1954 abdication crisis had ended: "Zaid's opinion is that for Shakhbut's disease, which is probably jealousy and parsimony in that order, there is no cure. He used to suggest [the appointment of] a British adviser, but I suspect that his mind is now turning to more drastic courses, involving retirement abroad for either Shakhbut or himself. However he has told me more than once that he has no intention of forcing the issue until the frontier dispute is finally settled, lest an open breach should invite the Saudis to exploit it."

An important step towards the resolution of the Buraimi Dispute would occur just over a year later, in September 1955, when the parties gathered in Geneva to argue their case in front of an international tribunal. The dispute would be judged by a five-member panel, including one British representative, one Saudi representative, and three independent appointees. The British legal team, representing the interests of both Abu Dhabi and Oman in the dispute, arrived in Switzerland armed with volumes of historical evidence to support their case. Sheikh Zayed and Sheikh Hazza also traveled to Geneva to give evidence in person.

However, the commencement of the long-awaited proceedings would end up being delayed for six days when one of the independent members of the tribunal failed to show up. He blamed it on a scheduling mix-up, but his subsequent admission that he could not travel from his home in Pakistan to Geneva right away because he had only just returned there from Saudi Arabia raised eyebrows.

When the hearing finally got underway, it quickly became clear that one of the main allegations at the heart of the British case was that Saudi officials had been bribing residents of the disputed territories to back their claims of sovereignty in the area. In his own evidence to the hearing, a reportedly nervous Sheikh Zayed revealed that he himself had been offered multiple bribes to betray his family and drop his own objections to the Saudi land claim, all of which he had refused. Sheikh Hazza did likewise.

However, as the arbitration unfolded, members of the British delegation in Geneva became increasingly concerned that the process had been rigged against them. In a feat of ethical contortionism, British officials complained repeatedly in the hearing room that the Saudi representative on the five-member tribunal was not fulfilling his duties in a sufficiently impartial manner, while privately expressing their own frustration that the British representative on the panel was not being equally partisan. When word filtered out that the tribunal was intending to dismiss the bribery allegations at the center of the case altogether, the British delegation quietly engineered the collapse of the arbitration process, including secretly recording one of the supposedly independent members of the tribunal admitting to accepting personal loans from the Saudi Government prior to his arrival in Geneva.

In the aftermath of this circus, it wasn't long before the British Government turned its attention to Plan B: Retaking the village of Hamasa by force. Shortly before daybreak on October 26, 1955, just weeks after the arbitration hearings had imploded in Geneva, the Trucial Oman Levies moved in. First, a force of around one hundred men surrounded and disarmed the fifteen-man Saudi Police Detachment that had been set up in the disputed territory near Buraimi, before its members were taken directly to the nearby airstrip to begin their journey back to Saudi Arabia. One shot was fired but no lives were lost in this part of the operation.

A second force went straight to the Omani village of Hamasa, where a gun battle erupted between the approaching Trucial Oman Levies and around two hundred tribesmen who had declared their loyalty to Saudi Arabia. As the battle ebbed and flowed throughout the morning, Sheikh Zayed and his brother Sheikh Hazza, who considered the clash in Hamasa to be the business of the Sultan of Muscat and Oman rather than their own, watched on through binoculars from the cover of the nearby dunes. With their help, though, contact was soon established between Edward Henderson, who had been mandated to represent the British Government on the ground that day, and the rebel leaders, and negotiations got underway that continued throughout the afternoon. Late that night, after a lengthy stalemate in the gun battle, the outnumbered leaders of the resistance finally surrendered and agreed to go into exile in Saudi Arabia.

The one-day battle claimed the lives of nine men, including two members of the Trucial Oman Levies. Documents and cash found in the early morning raid on the Saudi Police Detachment would later confirm British suspicions that the Saudis had indeed been bribing local residents for their support, just as had been alleged in Geneva.

In his book, *Arabian Destiny*, Henderson recounted witnessing two men emerging from the darkness and approaching Sheikh Zayed and Sheikh Hazza as they stood drinking coffee just hours after the battle in Hamasa had ended:

"As they approached Shaikh Zayed they went down on their knees in the sand and started to crawl towards him. Sheikh Hazza who was next to me whispered their names and I then realized that they were the two heads of families who alone of all the people of Abu Dhabi had joined the Saudis during the three years of their presence in Hamasa.

It was a dramatic moment and I was full of curiosity as to Sheikh Zayed's reaction. As the first one reached him, and seemed to be trying to kiss his feet, Shaikh Zayed with the natural dignity which is especially his, stooped, took him by the shoulders, raised him and said: "Peace be unto you. You are forgiven and you may return to your house in peace."

He did the like with the second. Both of them made for Shaikh Hazza who said with dignity in a soft voice.

'You heard the brother's word. Go to your homes. He has forgiven you.'"

The crisis was over, but the outcome of these events was less conclusive than it appeared. The Saudis may have been expelled from Hamasa, but the Kingdom had not abandoned its claim to a significant portion of Abu Dhabi territory. A messy abdication may have been averted, but Sheikh Shakhbut's reluctance to spend money would continue to frustrate progress in Abu Dhabi. In other words, the Buraimi Dispute may have ended, but the border issues that gave rise to it, and the fraternal fissures that it revealed, both remained dangerously unresolved. Neither situation could remain that way indefinitely.

— FIVE —

Arrested Development

After a slow start, the Trucial States Council becomes a catalyst for cooperation between the Rulers of the emirates. The discovery of oil in 1958 transforms Abu Dhabi's fortunes but the Ruler is reluctant to spend any of his newfound riches. Comparisons between the pace of development in Al Ain and Abu Dhabi become hard to ignore.

Shortly before 9:45 a.m. on November 8, 1955, just one week after the Trucial Oman Levies had conducted their dramatic raid on Hamasa, the Rulers of the seven Trucial States, accompanied by their deputies, crowded into a makeshift meeting room in the office of the British Political Agency in Dubai. This would be the eighth meeting of the Trucial States Council, formed by British officials three years earlier as a way to build trust between the ruling Sheikhs, to develop common rules and regulations that could be applied within each of their territories, and to stimulate much-needed social and economic development.

Although in hindsight it is tempting to think of the Trucial States Council as the original template for what would later become the United Arab Emirates, the truth is that the British officials behind the forum had no such ambitions at the time. In fact, in the months before the creation of the Council, and only two decades before the founding of the UAE, the British Resident in the Gulf privately assessed the long-term prospects of any meaningful integration between the emirates as follows: "As the Shaikhdoms develop, we might in due course persuade their governments to send representatives to some kind of council which would endeavor to achieve co-ordination in such matters as education, health, postal services, etc., but I am doubtful if we will be able to achieve any kind of political union under a central authority."

Even with these modest ambitions, it is fair to say that the Trucial States Council got off to an inauspicious start. The influential Rulers of Abu Dhabi and Dubai both failed to attend the first meeting in March 1952. When Sheikh Shakhbut finally did attend his first Trucial States Council meeting the following year, he appeared largely disinterested, with one British official speculating that he "tends to appreciate individual attention and does not entirely approve of the position of finding himself only one among six others of equal rank." At the fourth Trucial

States Council meeting hosted in Sharjah in November 1953, one elderly Ruler slept through the proceedings, and British officials were left with the distinct impression that the Sheikhs were only attending these twice-yearly gatherings out of courtesy to Her Majesty's Government.

However, by the time of the fifth meeting in July 1954, the atmosphere had mysteriously begun to change, even though nobody on the British side seemed to be able to work out why. The meeting was attended by all seven of the Trucial State Rulers, with the exception of the Ruler of Dubai, who was ably represented by his son, Sheikh Rashid bin Saeed Al Maktoum, who by this point was considered by many to be the de facto Ruler anyway. Sheikh Zayed, who was held in extremely high regard by British officials based on their dealings with him in Buraimi, also attended for the first time alongside his eldest brother. To the surprise of British officials, more than one Ruler came to the meeting armed with topics that they wanted to discuss, and the usually guarded group seemed more talkative and engaged than ever before.

Of course, even when people begin to talk, there is no guarantee that they will necessarily agree on anything. In his own analysis of the unusually lively meeting, the British Political Agent in Dubai noted:

"Even the Ruler of Abu Dhabi [Sheikh Shakhbut] whose bearing at the only previous meeting he had attended had been sphinx-like made several interventions in debate. Admittedly these were almost without exception to express opposition and dissent from the opinions of his colleagues, but his brother Shaikh Zaid subsequently explained that the Ruler had quarrelled with him on the journey to Dubai and the opinions expressed except in one instance were indicative more of general ill humour than the Ruler's real views which were known to vary from day to day. Shaikh Zaid took the opportunity privately to identify the State of Abu Dhabi wholeheartedly with the proceedings and decisions of the Council whatever its Ruler might have said to the contrary."

Later in the meeting, when the Ruler of Sharjah sought the advice of the group on how to deal with an issue that had arisen in relation to education, Sheikh Shakhbut expressed his astonishment at the question, adding that such a situation could not possibly arise in Abu Dhabi because "Abu Dhabi did not have such things as schools." When a British official suggested that this was not necessarily a good thing, Sheikh Shakhbut said simply that he agreed, without further explanation. By the middle of the 1950s, the lack of even minimal development in Abu Dhabi was puzzling to many observers, since by that point the Ruler had been receiving a steady stream of oil concession payments for more than fifteen years.

Despite his combative attitude at the meeting, which according to one observer "caused genuine amusement to his fellows and quite possibly to himself," Sheikh Shakhbut's standing offer to allocate four percent of any of Abu Dhabi's future oil revenues to the Trucial States

Council for development projects had undoubtedly given the body some much-needed local legitimacy, even though no oil had yet been found in Abu Dhabi, and there was no guarantee that it ever would be. Regardless, a portion of the potential funds had already been eagerly earmarked by the Rulers for the construction of hospitals and roads. The unspoken reality was that even if oil was found in Abu Dhabi, it would take years before the first barrel could be removed from the ground and exported. The question on the minds of British officials was what the Rulers intended to do in the meantime.

At the eighth meeting in November 1955, one British Political Agent tiptoed into the minefield of tribal politics to suggest that the Rulers should consider the introduction of taxes on some of their wealthier citizens in order to help fund the development of their territories:

"The Chairman was concerned at the absence of any significant contributions to the States' revenues by Trucial States inhabitants. They often earned considerable wages, yet did not contribute to improvements in the States. He recognized that local custom demanded that a Ruler should provide for his people from his own resources. These resources were, however, small and few Rulers could afford to initiate even modest improvements in their States. Were they to remain dependent on gifts from outside, for any advance in the conditions of their States? Or were they to remain passive until the discovery of oil in Abu Dhabi, or elsewhere on the Trucial Coast, transformed the picture? In any case, could they remain passive? Everywhere he went, he met requests for better schools, more medical attention and so on."

In the conversations that he was having at his *majlis* in Al Ain, and during his travels to other parts of Abu Dhabi territory, Sheikh Zayed had been hearing the same message from his own constituents. These rising expectations were inevitable. Oil had been discovered in Bahrain in 1932, Saudi Arabia and Kuwait in 1938, and Qatar in 1940, allowing these territories to leap ahead on the path to development. With an estimated sixteen thousand Trucial States citizens spending at least some time each year working abroad in the oil-rich Gulf states by the mid-1950s, local people were more aware than ever before of just how much they didn't have. Sheikh Zayed had experienced the same revelation himself when he had visited Europe in the early 1950s, and seen the schools, hospitals, museums and public parks of cities such as London and Paris, later recalling that: "There were a lot of dreams I was dreaming about our land catching up with the modern world, but I was not able to do anything because I did not have the wherewithal in my hands to achieve these dreams. I was sure, however, that one day they would become true."

In January 1958, Sheikh Zayed would lose his brother, Sheikh Hazza, after a lengthy battle with cancer. The two had been close, and in the final year of Sheikh Hazza's life, Sheikh Zayed had accompanied him to both New York City and India to receive hospital treatments at a time when comparable medical facilities were not available in the Trucial States. Known for his cheerfulness and his expertise in local tribal affairs, Sheikh Hazza had also shared his younger brother Sheikh Zayed's passion for nature and the outdoors, and the two had often hunted together with their falcons.

Less than ten weeks after Sheikh Hazza's passing, on the evening of March 28, 1958, the future of the Trucial States would be irreversibly changed with the discovery of commercial quantities of oil off the coast of Abu Dhabi. After decades of fruitless searching, oil would also be found in Abu Dhabi's onshore territory two years later. Although the first oil exports would not begin until 1962, Abu Dhabi was now on the path to becoming an energy powerhouse, and Sheikh Zayed wasted no time in moving to accelerate the social and economic development of the limited parts of the emirate that were under his control.

In 1959, the first government school in Al Ain, the Al Nahyaniah School for Boys, opened to the public, staffed primarily by teachers from Jordan. Sheikh Zayed's eldest son, and the future Ruler of Abu Dhabi and President of the UAE, Sheikh Khalifa, who had previously been educated exclusively by private tutors at Qasr Al Muwaiji, was one of the first students enrolled. The school had to be surrounded with barbed wire to prevent curious livestock from entering the building.

Also in 1959, Sheikh Zayed and Sheikh Shakhbut invited the American doctors, Pat Kennedy, Marian Kennedy and Raymond Joyce, to establish the first hospital on Abu Dhabi territory in Al Ain. Opened in 1960, and temporarily housed in a mud brick guest house, the makeshift Oasis Hospital provided the local population with access to modern healthcare services for the first time.

In her memoir, Gertrude Dycke, who left her home in Canada at the age of twenty-eight to join Oasis Hospital in 1963 before working there for the next thirty-eight years, provided a glimpse into the still-primitive nature of life in Al Ain around this time:

"In the village, the locals would sleep on the roof-top of their houses, if they had a mud-block house, or in the yard if it was a palm-stick house. Then they would usually build a platform, called a *manaama*, about a foot or two high, on which they would put their mattresses to avoid the snakes or scorpions on the ground. But the people out in the deserts just put their mats out on the sand and slept there. And nearly every night someone would come to the hospital with a scorpion sting, or even a snake bite. In 1963, everyone slept outside. We'd pull the sheets over our heads to keep out the sand and the sand-flies. Our beds were right out in the open, as we had no wall around the hospital at that time. Before dawn the Bedouin would be on the move already, often going right past us with their camels and yapping dogs."

With the restored and expanded *aflaj* network now bringing reliable supplies of water to the local oases, in 1962, Sheikh Zayed recruited Abdul Hafeez Khan, then a young agricultural scientist from Pakistan who was still completing his graduate studies in Beirut, to advise on the development of the local agricultural sector with a view to turning Al Ain green. Khan would live in Al Ain for the next fifty-eight years, and in what must be an eternal mystery to the local bird population, his former garden still contains an imported Australian eucalyptus tree planted by Sheikh Zayed in 1962.

Later that decade, Sheikh Zayed oversaw the establishment of a landmark captive breeding program for the Arabian oryx (a species of antelope native to the Arabian Peninsula) in Al Ain as part of a coordinated international effort that would help save the species from extinction, laying the groundwork for its successful reintroduction into the wild in the 1980s. He would eventually create a dedicated wildlife sanctuary on Abu Dhabi's Sir Bani Yas Island that, among other things, is currently home to one of the largest herds of Arabian oryx in the world.

In around 1960, Sheikh Zayed established a new family home in the Al Ain Palace, on the fringe of the Al Ain Oasis, following his marriage to Sheikha Fatima bint Mubarak Al Ketbi. Born in Al Hayer, in the Al Ain region, Sheikha Fatima would go on to become known as the Mother of the Nation and a prominent advocate for women and families in the UAE.

In the middle of the Al Ain Palace compound, Sheikh Zayed had two formal *majlises* built, one right on top of the other. They are still there today. The downstairs room was set up like a traditional *majlis*, with cushions laid out on the floor. The upstairs room looked much the same, except it was furnished with couches, armchairs and coffee tables, so that the increasing number of foreign visitors coming to meet with Sheikh Zayed in the early 1960s could do so without sitting on the floor, which they were not accustomed to.

One of those visitors, J.P. Tripp, the former British Political Agent in Dubai, reported back to the Foreign Office in London on the astounding progress that he had witnessed on a recent trip to Al Ain in 1962. Under Sheikh Zayed's leadership, a thriving new market had been established and was attracting merchants from great distances away, the flow of water to support the growth of agriculture in Al Ain and its surrounding villages had tripled in recent years, and around seventy boys were enrolled at the local school. By this point, the Oasis Hospital had also been up and running for more than two years.

Meanwhile, on the coast, it was as if nothing had changed. The sweltering town of Abu Dhabi was frozen in time. The biggest development project to be completed in Abu Dhabi was the construction of the town's first road in 1960, but this was the exception that proved the rule: It was built by stealth while Sheikh Shakhbut was out of the country and Sheikh Zayed was serving in his place as Acting Ruler.

In his book, *From Rags to Riches*, Mohammed Al-Fahim described the chronic uncertainty that prevailed in the town of Abu Dhabi in the years after the discovery of oil:

"In 1960 the inhabitants still lived from hand to mouth. Incomes were far below the poverty line; many people went hungry and some even resorted to hunting lizards and dhubs [a form of spiny-tailed lizard] to feed themselves and their families. There were no medical facilities to treat the sick and the first non-religious school, ill-equipped as it was, had only opened the previous year. Nevertheless, we saw signs with our own eyes that indicated we should be moving forward. We witnessed an increase in the number of foreigners in Abu Dhabi as well as an upsurge in the movement of oil-related equipment and heavy trucks. New companies set up camps in the desert and on Das Island and hired locals to work for them as drivers, watchmen and labourers. We all knew oil had been discovered. There was a general atmosphere of expectation. Yet there was no confirmation of the discovery from the Ruler's office or even from the Ruler himself. Privately, Abu Dhabians had many questions: Was the discovery significant? What would it mean for us? How would our lives be changed? Who would manage the development that would surely be taking place soon?"

It would take another six years, but in August 1966, the people of Abu Dhabi would finally get their answer.

— SIX —
Succession

Sheikh Shakhbut's reluctance to invest in the development of Abu Dhabi confounds international observers and frustrates his family. Concerns grow over how Abu Dhabi's burgeoning oil wealth is being managed and deployed. In August 1966, senior members of the ruling Al Nahyan family remove Sheikh Shakhbut from power and appoint Sheikh Zayed as the new Ruler of Abu Dhabi.

Archie Lamb was thinking ahead. On January 19, 1966, Lamb, then the British Political Agent in Abu Dhabi, wrote to his boss in Bahrain to alert him to the fact that in two years' time, Sheikh Shakhbut bin Sultan Al Nahyan would have been the Ruler of Abu Dhabi for 40 years. Lamb thought that the British Government should mark the occasion by inviting Sheikh Shakhbut to London for an official visit, and recommended that the planning for such an event should begin right away.

What stands out most about Lamb's letter is just how confident he was that Sheikh Shakhbut would still be in power two years later ("... I see nothing around me or in the health of Shakhbut to suggest that he will not."). Within seven months, Sheikh Shakhbut would have been peacefully removed from power by his own family and replaced as the Ruler of Abu Dhabi by his forty-eight-year-old brother, Sheikh Zayed.

In fairness to Lamb, he was well aware that there had been rising speculation in both Abu Dhabi and London about the prospect of Sheikh Zayed eventually succeeding Sheikh Shakhbut, and doing for the emirate as a whole what he had done in Al Ain over the previous two decades. However, he also knew better than anyone that Sheikh Zayed had consistently resisted calls for him to usurp his eldest brother. What Lamb failed to see coming was Sheikh Zayed's change of heart.

He may not have been alone. As late as June 1966, just two months before Sheikh Shakhbut was ousted in a bloodless palace coup, Sheikh Zayed himself continued to insist that he would not move against his brother, and lashed out at British officials for suggesting that he should contemplate doing so. That's not to suggest that Sheikh Zayed was reluctant to take the job, or that he doubted he was the right man to lead Abu Dhabi into the future. Far from it. Rather, he appears to have been hoping that his brother would eventually step aside voluntarily, rather than needing to be forced out. Deep down, though, he probably knew that was never going to happen.

The pressure to make a change had been building in Abu Dhabi for at least a decade. By the early 1950s, Sheikh Shakhbut's reluctance to spend money had already become an intense source of frustration to his family and others around him. Indeed, this had been the trigger for the aborted abdication crisis of 1954. Unable to alter the Ruler's cautious outlook, his brothers had eventually accepted it as just one of his eccentricities, and did their best to work around it. Sheikh Zayed did what he could to improve living conditions in Al Ain with the limited resources that he had at his disposal. The people of Abu Dhabi simply got on with their lives, or left to seek opportunities elsewhere. However, the discovery of oil in 1958 and Abu Dhabi's stunning new financial reality changed everything. Sheikh Shakhbut still had time to change, but the clock was ticking now and could not be stopped.

Rather than spur him into action, though, the heightened expectations only seemed to stiffen the Ruler's resistance to the idea of investing his newfound riches in the development of Abu Dhabi. In 1963, a disturbing profile in an American magazine described an eccentric Sheikh Shakhbut (on his way to becoming "the world's richest man") holding court in his *majlis* at Qasr Al Hosn three times a day, his guests seated on battered old sofas and armchairs, waiting patiently for their chance to pitch the Ruler one grand scheme after another, nearly all of which would be rejected in a whisper. It sounds apocryphal, and probably was, but according to the unflattering piece, although he appeared to have no interest in the building of roads and hospitals, the wealthy Ruler would gladly spend hours arguing over the price of onions for his soup. While hosting a recent British trade delegation for lunch, he had allegedly served his guests bowls of Jell-O without spoons, because he had steadfastly refused to approve the purchasing of any cutlery. Exaggerated or not, it all sounded a little strange.

Alarmingly, in addition to the lack of development at home, Sheikh Shakhbut was also beginning to adopt a more isolationist policy in relation to his closest neighbors, including backing away from his earlier commitment to allocate four percent of any future oil revenues to the Trucial States Council, where it could be used to fund development projects in the other six member states. He would eventually threaten to withdraw from the Trucial States Council altogether, potentially unraveling the single most important effort to promote greater cooperation between the emirates, and undermining Abu Dhabi's own security interests in the process.

Two years before the eventual succession, the prospect of a potential leadership change in Abu Dhabi was secretly being discussed at the highest levels in London. In December of 1964, then British Prime Minister, Harold Wilson, was handed a secret memo on the potential implications of Sheikh Zayed hypothetically replacing Sheikh Shakhbut as the Ruler of Abu Dhabi, including his likely attitude to sharing oil revenues and considering a federation with the other Trucial States. Although British officials in the Gulf were hesitant to predict with any certainty what Sheikh Zayed might do if he took the reins, they left the Prime Minister in no doubt that " . . . so long as Sheikh Shakhbut is the Ruler, federation including Abu Dhabi, which is the only state with any substantial revenue, is out of the question, and there is no sign of his being ready to give any assistance to the other States." However, apart from some gentle prodding behind the scenes, there is no evidence that they decided to do anything about it. In a seemingly uncharacteristic show of restraint, British officials appear to have been content to wait until members of the ruling family reached the same conclusion that they had.

It was only a matter of time. On February 13, 1966, Archie Lamb received an unexpected visit from the Ruler's brother, Sheikh Khalid. Sheikh Khalid had come alone, and the two would speak in private for the next ninety minutes. The atmosphere was grim. According to Lamb, his visitor had come to warn him that he should put no faith in Sheikh Shakhbut's recent assurances that he would assemble a competent government administration and accelerate the pace of development in Abu Dhabi. He had no intention of changing anything, and would continue to let the money pile up in the bank. Lamb listened intently to Sheikh Khalid's warnings, but reading between the lines, he went to bed that night with the unshakeable feeling that the Ruler of Abu Dhabi was losing the support of his own family.

From the perspective of the British Government, this was a welcome development, but one that needed to be handled with care. Although British officials in the Gulf had developed a grudging respect for Sheikh Shakhbut over the years, who was still being described in confidential briefing documents around this time as a man of considerable charm and intelligence, his erratic personality and hostile attitude to development continued to confound them. In one memorable example, after agreeing to take delivery of a prefabricated hospital in 1963, Sheikh Shakhbut inexplicably insisted that the parts remain in their crates for three years before allowing the hospital to be assembled. Even then, he refused to order any medical equipment to go inside it. Sometimes he would reluctantly approve development projects, only to abruptly cancel them after the plans had been drawn up, as he did in relation to the construction of a jetty and crucial electricity projects in April 1966.

However, in the same month that he canceled those projects, Sheikh Shakhbut may have also inadvertently triggered his own demise. During a high-profile state visit abroad, he pledged extravagant gifts to the people of Jordan that were clearly worth far more than he was spending on development projects at home. It would later be discovered that he had made an even more generous financial gift to the King of Jordan personally. When word of the Ruler's lavish generosity filtered back to Abu Dhabi, it alarmed

British officials and infuriated members of the ruling family. The imbalance could not be justified, and raised legitimate concerns about how Abu Dhabi's growing oil wealth was being managed and deployed. In hindsight, it may well have been the final straw.

By this point, the ruling family of Abu Dhabi had a lot to lose. Since oil exports began in 1962, the amount of money flowing into the Ruler's coffers had increased exponentially. In 1963, Sheikh Shakhbut received £2.25m in oil revenue. In 1965, this figure had risen to £10.75m. In 1966, the amount was projected to climb to a staggering £25m. However, in the four years between 1962 and 1966, only £2m was spent on development projects, yielding a few roads, one jetty, one water distillation plant, two schools, one power station, and a pipe to transfer water from Al Ain to Abu Dhabi. It was obviously better than nothing, but nowhere near enough considering the low base that Abu Dhabi was starting from.

In May 1966, Sheikh Zayed and Sheikh Khalid, along with their cousin, Sheikh Muhammed bin Khalifa, devised a plan to pressure Sheikh Shakhbut to provide them with greater visibility into how he was managing Abu Dhabi's finances. Among other things, they wanted to know how much money was being paid out in allowances to members of the royal family each month, and how much could be made available for development projects that would benefit the people of Abu Dhabi. The ad hoc bookkeeping practices of the past were no longer acceptable for the huge sums of money that were now involved. The surplus oil revenue could not be allowed to sit idle, or be frittered away, when there was so much that needed to be done.

Banding together, they refused to accept any further payments from the Ruler until he agreed to create a proper budget for Abu Dhabi. Sheikh Shakhbut responded indignantly and accused his closest relatives of conspiring against him. He refused their demand for him to institute a budget, but reluctantly agreed to grant Sheikh Zayed additional powers as the President of the Department of Finance to sign checks and make certain spending decisions on his behalf. A few weeks later, he provided his brothers with a list of the seventy-three family members to whom he was paying allowances. This put an end to the argument, but didn't really solve the problem, and the can was kicked a little further down the road. Meanwhile, inside Qasr Al Hosn, an increasingly mistrustful Sheikh Shakhbut had the two office safes moved into his private quarters, where he could keep a closer eye on them. It wasn't a good sign.

A few days later, on June 7, 1966, Sheikh Zayed departed Abu Dhabi and traveled to the UK for a long-planned family holiday, and so that one of his sons could receive medical treatment. British officials in the Gulf urged him to delay his trip for a few weeks so that he could be in Abu Dhabi for the visit of the outgoing Political Resident, who planned to confront Sheikh Shakhbut about the slow pace of development occurring under his watch. Sheikh Zayed refused this request, indicating that if British officials intended to be firm with his brother, then they should do so in private rather than with him present.

After landing in the UK, Sheikh Zayed joined his family at Hall Barn, a country house in Beaconsfield, built by a fellow poet and politician in around 1675. During his stay, he was the guest of honor at a garden party, went to Ascot on multiple occasions to see horses, and attended a hovercraft show in Hampshire, with a view to potentially procuring some of these futuristic new amphibious vehicles for the emerging Abu Dhabi Defence Force. However, the timing of the visit, which also included a mysterious private meeting at the Foreign and Commonwealth Office in London, would later come back to haunt him, and fuel suspicions in the region that the removal of Sheikh Shakhbut had been an elaborate British plot.

It wasn't an outlandish theory. There is no doubt that by 1966, the British Government would have preferred to be dealing with Sheikh Zayed as the Ruler of Abu Dhabi. This is hardly surprising. By this point, he had been a reliable partner to British officials in the Gulf for more than fifteen years. He was determined to accelerate the social and economic development of Abu Dhabi, he welcomed British advice, and he was committed to supporting the work of the Trucial States Council and exploring greater integration between its member states. By all accounts, he was also more personable and charismatic than his brother, and seemed more equipped to provide stable and effective leadership to his own people.

However, the idea that this led to Sheikh Zayed being 'installed' by the British Government ignores the fact that the majority of people in Abu Dhabi, including within the ruling family itself, had long supported the idea of him taking over too, in large part based on what he had accomplished in Al Ain. That is why, when it finally happened, the general reaction of the people of Abu Dhabi was reportedly one of relief, not rage. Did the British Government have a hand in Sheikh Zayed's accession in August 1966? Without a doubt; but that is not the same as engineering it.

In the end, nobody did more to bring Sheikh Shakhbut's rule to an end than the man himself. While Sheikh Zayed was still in the UK, alarming reports began to emerge of disloyal chatter that had been picked up within the ranks of the newly-created Abu Dhabi Defence Force over unpaid wages. British officials were skeptical that anything would come of these grumblings, but were concerned that the existence of "a trained and efficient body of men with a grudge against the Ruler" could be taken advantage of by outside agitators. Ultimately, it was just one more example of the Ruler's grip on the purse strings undermining his own interests and getting in the way of his ability to run the state.

After almost two months away, Sheikh Zayed returned to Abu Dhabi from the UK at the end of July. When word spread that he was back, the people of Al Ain spontaneously spilled out onto the streets to welcome him home. They didn't know it, but this would be the last time that they would ever greet him as the Ruler's Representative to the area. The following week, members of the ruling family would decide behind closed doors to put Sheikh Zayed in charge of the affairs of Abu Dhabi as a whole. Sheikh Zayed agreed that the time had come to make a change, but consistent with the pledge that he had made to his mother as a child, he resolved to make the transition a peaceful one.

"Frankly I didn't wish, or desire, the responsibility," he would later claim, reflecting on the difficult decision to replace his brother. "What made me accept it? It was only my realisation of the losses the people were suffering. I felt in the end that I should allow myself to be convinced that I accept the responsibility . . . It had [also] reached a point when I had to satisfy my conscience that my brother would not only remain in good health, but also that others would not take advantage of his predicament."

On August 4, 1966, senior members of the ruling Al Nahyan family delivered the following letter to the British Government's Acting Political Resident in Abu Dhabi:

"Impelled by lamentable condition of our country and by misrule, inefficiency, mental instability of Sheikh Shakhbut and his rejection of all advice, we, Heads and lawful representatives of Ruling family have decided to depose him and have elected Sheikh Zaid in his place.

Our object being to avoid bloodshed and disturbance of peace we request Her Majesty's Government to give us their support and remove Shakhbut permanently, and his sons Said and Sultan temporarily, to the country they wish at our expense."

The British Government acknowledged the decision and indicated that it was prepared to deal with Sheikh Zayed as the legitimate Ruler of Abu Dhabi. Two days later, on August 6, 1966, the Acting Political Resident in the Gulf visited Sheikh Shakhbut just after 11:00 a.m. and notified him of the British Government's intention to respect his family's wishes and to facilitate his removal from Abu Dhabi. Blind in one eye, and losing his sight in the other, a defiant Sheikh Shakhbut initially refused to go, and Sheikh Zayed ended up speaking to his brother by phone for almost an hour from the nearby Police Head-quarters, explaining the family's decision and urging him to leave the palace peacefully.

Eventually, the outgoing Ruler accepted his fate, and after exiting the palace through a military guard of honor arranged at the request of Sheikh Zayed, he was escorted to a waiting aircraft by the Trucial Oman Scouts and flown to Bahrain by the British Royal Air Force. His immediate family followed shortly after on a separate plane chartered by Sheikh Zayed. After thirty-eight years in power, Sheikh Shakhbut's reign had been peacefully brought to a close in less than three days.

Later that night, though, something curious happened on the streets of Abu Dhabi. Anticipating unrest once people learned that their longtime Ruler had been forcibly removed from office and sent into exile, the British

Government had deployed two squadrons of Trucial Oman Scouts to maintain law and order in the town. The troops waited through the night, but no backlash ever came.

— SEVEN —
Aftermath

Sheikh Zayed's accession is broadly welcomed throughout the emirate and the Gulf as he outlines plans for the long-overdue development of Abu Dhabi and the deepening of its ties with the other Trucial States. Relations with the neighboring Ruler of Dubai get off to a rocky start.

In the days after he became the Ruler of Abu Dhabi in August 1966, Sheikh Zayed believed that his life was in danger. He barely left the confines of his palace for a week, where his private quarters were guarded round the clock. The new Ruler's concerns for his own safety were not entirely unfounded, but as it turned out, the reaction to the leadership change across Abu Dhabi was fairly muted, with the mood throughout the emirate that week described as one of quiet relief, but not outward jubilation.

Even as he remained isolated, within two days of coming to power, Sheikh Zayed announced transformative plans for the long-awaited development of Abu Dhabi, and indicated that once the immediate needs of his own people had been met, he would also begin providing financial aid to poorer states in the Gulf. Over the next two weeks, he distributed millions of dollars in direct cash payments to the residents of Abu Dhabi and its neighboring towns, as well as members of the local Bedouin population, many of whom had been struggling to make ends meet for as long as they could remember. As word spread, thousands of people made the trip to Qasr Al Hosn and waited patiently in line to receive their own gift.

The new Ruler also initiated the long-overdue process of building a modern government structure to oversee the running of the emirate, including the establishment of dedicated departments in areas such as health, education, water, electricity, labor, public works, agriculture, finance and the law, along with the introduction of an annual budget process. It was a dramatic change in tone, and sent a clear signal to the people of Abu Dhabi that a new and more professional era of governance had begun.

Although his accession had been broadly welcomed throughout the emirate, Sheikh Zayed knew that the jury was still out on his ability to deliver on his promises. "The only way to create confidence was in fact to put the State itself on probation," he would later say of his early days as the Ruler of Abu Dhabi. "I felt that only by establishing a probationary period would people discover that the edifice being erected before their eyes was built on rock, not sand. Man can only believe what he may touch and feel."

Outside of the Trucial States, the regional reaction to Sheikh Zayed's rise to power was mixed, but still broadly positive. The Government of Bahrain, which was now playing host to the exiled former Ruler of Abu Dhabi and his thirty-strong entourage, demanded multiple assurances from British officials that his removal had indeed been at the behest of the ruling family. The only complaint from the Government of Kuwait was that it hadn't happened sooner. Officials in Saudi Arabia cautiously welcomed the change, but were mostly focused on understanding the impact that it could have on their lingering border dispute with Abu Dhabi.

The strongest objection came from right next door. Sheikh Rashid, now the Ruler of Dubai, lodged a formal protest with the British Government over its involvement in the affair, and was soon actively lobbying the Rulers of both Bahrain and Qatar to join him in a public protest over the incident. In 1966, Dubai was more developed than Abu Dhabi, had a larger population, and the opinion of its Ruler carried a lot of political weight within the Trucial States. Commercial quantities of oil had only been discovered in its offshore territory earlier that year, but even without it, Sheikh Rashid had successfully turned Dubai into a vibrant trading hub with roads, water, electricity, a busy port, an international airport, a growing banking sector, a functioning municipality, a professional police force, and even a public library.

He also commanded the respect of British officials in the region, who admired his leadership style and his commercial acumen. "He lives simply and works hard," wrote one British official in a confidential analysis of the Dubai Ruler prepared around this time. "Sheikh Rashid has made a major contribution to Dubai's prosperity by creating what he believes to be the optimum conditions for maximum trade. He is laissez-faire in his attitude, believing in encouraging merchants to come to Dubai and allowing them to conduct their activities with a minimum of Governmental interference. A matching contribution has been Rashid's development of the basic infrastructure of a modern town." Buried in the same set of briefing materials was a knowing warning: "Sheikh Rashid does not speak English but he understands more than he admits."

Despite his reputation for independence, the strident position taken by Sheikh Rashid in the aftermath of Sheikh Zayed's accession was surprising to some, because it was well known that he had not been particularly close with the former Ruler of Abu Dhabi. However, it soon became apparent that what he really objected to was not the change in leadership itself, but the involvement of the Trucial Oman Scouts, which operated under British command. In his view, their participation in the deposal of the former Ruler of Abu Dhabi had undermined their impartiality, and left the other Trucial State Rulers with the impression that the British Government could remove any one of them should it choose to do so in the future. It certainly could not be relied upon to come to their aid. More than four decades later, a new generation of leaders in the UAE would be echoing this sentiment in relation to the Obama administration's response to anti-government protests in Egypt in 2011.

On August 20, 1966, two weeks after he had come to power, Sheikh Zayed met face-to-face in Abu Dhabi with Sheikh Rashid and Sheikh Khalifa bin Salman, the brother of the Emir of Bahrain, in an attempt to clear the air. The atmosphere was cordial but tense. However, rather than getting straight down to business, the three Sheikhs first endured what must have been a fairly awkward lunch before anybody brought up the elephant in the room. When the time came, Sheikh Rashid took the opportunity to explain his concerns with the manner in which power had recently changed hands in Abu Dhabi, and specifically with the perceived role of the British Government in the process.

Sheikh Zayed listened patiently before assuring his guests that the decision to make a leadership change had been made by the ruling family alone. He added that it was a decision that they had spent years hoping to avoid. He also said that, contrary to what his dining companions may have heard, only words, not force, were used to remove his brother from the Ruler's palace, and he offered to produce eyewitnesses to verify his account. Sheikh Rashid indicated that this would not be necessary.

Sheikh Zayed then brought up the subject of the proposed public protest and pointed out that it would be interpreted by many as a protest against him, not against the British Government, and would therefore be seized upon by others in the region who wished to exploit it for propaganda purposes. He said that if his guests still had concerns over the nature of his accession, they were entitled to continue raising them, but he urged them to refrain from airing their dirty laundry in public. In what could easily have been interpreted as a threat, he indicated that the taking of such a path would represent a parting of the ways with Abu Dhabi. Mollified for the time being, Sheikh Rashid reportedly signaled his assent by replying "Yasir, Yastawwi" ("Alright, that goes"), before expressing a desire for friendship with his fellow Ruler. The protest was off, but the lack of trust between the leaders of Abu Dhabi and Dubai was palpable.

Things would get worse before they got better. Within weeks of his accession, Sheikh Zayed agreed to make an initial contribution of £500,000 to the Trucial States Development Fund, which had been created a year earlier to serve as the dedicated development arm of the Trucial States Council. Sheikh Zayed would quadruple this contribution over the course of his first two years in office. At the same time, though, it was an open secret that he was also providing direct financial assistance to the Rulers of the poorer northern emirates, outside of the official channels of the Trucial States Council. The extra assistance was certainly welcome. In 1966, the main source of revenue of the five northern emirates came from the sale of their own official postage stamps to collectors. British officials repeatedly urged Sheikh Zayed to desist from making these side payments, out of fear that they would only deepen the mistrust that was emerging between him and Sheikh Rashid, but he consistently brushed off their concerns, arguing that he had every right to put money directly into his neighbors' pockets if he wished to do so.

Unsurprisingly, Sheikh Rashid perceived these payments to the northern emirates precisely as British officials expected. The steady movement of people from Dubai to Abu Dhabi, including many former Abu Dhabi residents who had left during poorer times but were now seeking to return, did little to ease his concerns. When a group of Bedouin tribesmen abruptly switched their allegiance from Dubai to Abu Dhabi, Sheikh Rashid ordered the Head of the Dubai Police Department to write to his counterpart in Abu Dhabi to demand the collection and return of the rifles that he had given to the defectors some years earlier.

However, the biggest source of tension between Abu Dhabi and Dubai throughout 1967 was the fact that the border between the two emirates had never been settled, and its final placement would determine the ownership of a number of oil wells. The resources in question were of relatively greater economic importance to Dubai, and correspondence from the period suggests that Sheikh Zayed may have been more willing to compromise on the border issue than it appeared at the time, but members of his family were urging him to take a harder line.

Even at the height of these tensions, the two Rulers would both privately admit to British officials that they actually had a lot of respect for each other. They weren't particularly effusive with their praise – in one exchange around this time, Sheikh Zayed is merely quoted as saying that Sheikh Rashid is "a man," while in another, Sheikh Rashid reportedly says that Sheikh Zayed is "a good man" – but they appear to have intuitively understood from the beginning that their fates were intertwined. Their rivalry may have simmered over the years, but they never allowed it to boil over.

According to one British official who knew both men well, "The difference between them I think is the inevitable difference between a country gentleman who has come into a vast estate and is of a warm and generous nature, and man who, although capable of considerable generosity when called upon, has been engaged in a perpetual rat-race for as long as anyone can remember, and whose nerves and energies are correspondingly taut." The two Rulers also had very different leadership styles, with one British Government analysis noting that "while Sheikh Zaid of Abu Dhabi rules essentially as a tribal chieftain, Sheikh Rashid's methods resemble those of a Renaissance merchant prince."

For all of their apparent differences, though, the similarities between them are striking. Although Sheikh Rashid was slightly older (a fact that was not lost on Sheikh Zayed, who once reminded British officials that he considered Sheikh Rashid to be his elder), the two Rulers had been born within six years of each other, roughly on either side of World War I. Both of their fathers had served as the Rulers of their respective emirates, and they are each said to have learned the art of leadership by spending time among the adults in the *majlis* from an early age. They are also both said to have been heavily influenced by their mothers, Sheikha Salama and Sheikha Hessa. They shared a lifelong passion for falconry and hunting, were both accomplished horse riders in their youth, and for the remainder of their lives, they were consistently described by those that knew them as being at their most relaxed and comfortable in the desert. They also had a natural affinity with and enjoyed the respect of the local Bedouin tribes in their respective territories.

Both described as hands-on leaders, Sheikh Zayed and Sheikh Rashid independently gained a reputation for turning up unannounced on construction sites early in the morning, for working tirelessly late into the evening, for being across even the most minor details of individual projects, and perhaps most uncannily, for their shared habit of overcoming the language barrier with non-Arab advisors by drawing their development plans into the sand with their camel sticks. They were also both devout

Muslims that displayed a high degree of cultural and religious tolerance, including allocating land within their respective emirates for the construction of churches and other non-Muslim houses of worship, long before there was any political benefit in doing so. Finally, despite having received very limited formal schooling of their own, they both placed great emphasis on the importance of education, with Sheikh Zayed literally paying families to send their children to school in Abu Dhabi, and Sheikh Rashid allowing his own palace to be used as an elementary school during the cooler months of the year in Dubai. In hindsight, they might actually have had more in common than their British interlocutors realized, and it was therefore perhaps inevitable that their own relationship would feature some occasional turbulence.

In May 1967, Sheikh Zayed reached out to Sheikh Rashid via an intermediary to propose a face-to-face meeting in Al Ain to resolve some of their differences. Sheikh Rashid controversially declined the meeting, and as speculation mounted that the Ruler of Dubai was contemplating taking the border dispute between the two emirates to international arbitration, British officials stepped up their own efforts to broker a settlement between the Rulers, whose relationship would be crucial to the long-term stability of the Trucial States.

The impact of these efforts was negligible, with one of the biggest breakthroughs being the establishment of a direct backchannel between the two Rulers via Sheikh Maktoum bin Rashid Al Maktoum (Sheikh Rashid's son, who would later succeed him as the Ruler of Dubai and Vice President of the UAE). There were other signs of a potential thawing. By the end of 1967, Sheikh Rashid was secretly tipping Sheikh Zayed off about supposed efforts to undermine him and privately counseling him to assert greater authority in the running of his own government. In reality, though, a lasting sea change in their relationship would not come until the following year, when the British Government would announce that it was permanently withdrawing from the region.

There appeared to be no misgivings within the emirate of Abu Dhabi itself, and by the time August 1967 rolled around, any controversy surrounding Sheikh Zayed's rise to power one year earlier had already been forgotten. For the people of Abu Dhabi, the previous twelve months had easily been the most productive and promising in living memory, and they were eager to celebrate the first anniversary of their Ruler's accession in style. It is fair to say that things got a little out of hand.

A week before the occasion, a series of ceremonial arches were erected over the main street of the town, and a large green obelisk was installed at the main intersection. The streets were lined with red and white barber's poles, and an alternating pattern of Abu Dhabi flags and photos of the Ruler hung from a fourteen-mile-long piece of string.

The striped poles had been embellished with multi-colored bunches of lights, which eventually overloaded the local power supply and triggered a blackout.

According to the event program, the celebration was meant to begin with an orderly parade of military vehicles from the Abu Dhabi Defence Force. However, as the vehicles approached the Ruler's stand, the over-excited drivers reportedly began wildly accelerating, braking and weaving in and out of one another's paths, causing an unfortunate cameraman stationed in one of the vehicles to be flipped upside down. A series of extravagant floats commissioned by various companies doing business in Abu Dhabi soon followed down the main street, until one of them collided with one of the ceremonial arches and had to be disassembled before the procession could continue.

Unsatisfied with a mere parade float, one enthusiastic British engineering firm decided to mark the occasion by bringing a full-sized commercial airliner – a de Havilland Comet – to Abu Dhabi for the first time, against the advice of local aviation officials. When the heavier-than-usual aircraft landed on the town's unfinished runway, a billowing cloud of dust overwhelmed its engines, triggering the plane's fire alarms and terrifying the passengers aboard the ceremonial flight.

According to those in attendance, Sheikh Zayed appeared to enjoy the festivities, but it's possible that he was just being polite. His older brother, Sheikh Khalid, was reportedly less impressed by the ostentatious display, complaining that it was a gratuitous waste of money that would make Abu Dhabi look ridiculous in the eyes of the world. In hindsight, the people of the emirate may have been wise to celebrate when they had the chance. Less than six months after the poles and arches were taken down, the future of Abu Dhabi and the Trucial States would be thrown into disarray by a political decision made more than three thousand miles away.

— EIGHT —
Union in Theory

The British Government announces plans to withdraw from the Gulf. At a meeting in the desert, Sheikh Zayed and Sheikh Rashid reach a historic agreement to form a union between Abu Dhabi and Dubai as the potential nucleus of a wider federation. After efforts to create a nine-member union falter, the six-member United Arab Emirates comes into being on December 2, 1971. Ras Al Khaimah joins the union in February 1972.

———————

At noon on January 9, 1968, Sheikh Zayed hosted a meeting with Goronwy Roberts, the visiting UK Minister of State for Foreign Affairs, and four other senior British officials, at Qasr Al Hosn in Abu Dhabi. The last time they had met, Roberts had assured the Ruler of Abu Dhabi that despite the recent British withdrawal from Aden in November 1967, the UK Government had no intention of abandoning its longstanding treaty obligations to the Trucial States. On the contrary, a strong British presence would be retained in the Gulf for as long as it was necessary to maintain peace and stability in the area.

Now, just two months later, Roberts had returned to Abu Dhabi to inform Sheikh Zayed that the situation had changed. Contrary to what he had said previously, the UK Government had decided to withdraw its forces and personnel from the region by the end of 1971, regardless of what was happening on the ground. After 150 years under the British security umbrella, the Trucial States would soon be left to fend for themselves. The UK Prime Minister would announce the decision in a week's time.

Sheikh Zayed took the seismic news in his stride and assured his visitors that he had always understood that the British presence in the Gulf would one day come to an end. He said that he was less worried about the British decision to leave per se, and more concerned with how the withdrawal would be managed. He warned Roberts and his colleagues that if the British Government just packed up and departed without any thought for what they left behind, then the UK would permanently destroy its reputation in the area, especially among the people of the Trucial States. On the other hand, if they could help to unify some or all of the fragmented Gulf states on their way out the door, and create a system that enabled them to stand shoulder-to-shoulder with one another against external aggression, then the UK could always count on their friendship. He believed that such an outcome was possible, and that the people of the Trucial States wanted their Rulers to cooperate more fully with one another on security and development. One British official in the room would later describe Sheikh Zayed's reaction to the news as "curiously muted," and assert that his optimistic plans to forge stronger ties between the Trucial States were "probably unrealistic."

What British officials did not fully anticipate was the immediate and dramatic effect that the withdrawal decision would have on the historically complicated relationship between Sheikh Zayed and Sheikh Rashid. In hindsight, this should have been easy to see coming. The Rulers of Abu Dhabi and Dubai knew better than anyone just how ill-prepared the seven Trucial States were for independence, and with less than four years to get their houses in order, it was clearly in both of their interests to work together rather than against one another. After all, in 1968, the combined population of Abu Dhabi (46,500) and Dubai (59,000) represented around sixty percent of the population of the entire Trucial States (180,200), and this proportion was only expected to increase over time. If the two of them could agree on a way forward, then there was a good chance that the other Rulers would follow.

Within days of the withdrawal being announced in London, Sheikh Zayed received a message through an intermediary that Sheikh Rashid wanted to meet with him. He readily agreed, and the two men sat down together two days later in Al Ain on January 22, 1968. We don't know exactly what was said, but by the end of that two-hour meeting, Sheikh Zayed and Sheikh Rashid had agreed to put aside their personal and political differences in order to deepen the ties between Abu Dhabi and Dubai.

The details were yet to be worked out, but in a spirit of shared optimism, the two Rulers put out an enthusiastic but somewhat vague communique, espousing the values of "cooperation," "solidarity" and "common destiny," and Sheikh Zayed announced that he would immediately pave the road between Abu Dhabi and Dubai. Two days later, Sheikh Rashid would personally follow up with the UK Government on a delicate offer that Sheikh Zayed had made in his initial meeting with Goronwy Roberts, to cover the cost of maintaining a British military presence in the area beyond 1971 (the secret offer would ultimately be declined by the UK Government, but not before a member of the British cabinet would carelessly reveal its existence to the BBC). The path forward remained hazy, but the message was clear: Regardless of what had happened in the past, Sheikh Zayed and Sheikh Rashid were determined to travel in the same direction, albeit still in separate lanes.

It did not take long before those lanes began to merge. Less than one month after their meeting in Al Ain, Sheikh Zayed and Sheikh Rashid met again on February 18, 1968, this time at an impromptu campsite set up near Al Semih, at a place called Agoura Al Sedira, close to the border between Abu Dhabi and Dubai, to discuss the creation of a formal union between their two emirates. The historic deal was done with little fanfare, but the resulting bilateral agreement, known as the Union Accord, created the unlikely nucleus around which the United Arab Emirates would be formed more than three years later.

Under the terms of the Union Accord, Abu Dhabi and Dubai agreed to form a new federal state under one flag that would have overarching responsibility for policy in foreign affairs, defense and security, health and education, and citizenship and immigration. On the same day, the two Rulers settled a longstanding offshore boundary dispute between their emirates, largely in Dubai's favor, thus removing one of the biggest sources of tension in their relationship up to that point. Within days of the agreement, Sheikh Zayed also began subsidizing the provision of electricity to residents of Dubai at his own expense.

The initial plan was to expand the union quickly. Specifically, the Union Accord indicated that the Rulers of the other five Trucial States (Sharjah, Ras Al Khaimah, Fujairah, Umm Al Quwain and Ajman) would be invited to *discuss* and *participate* in the union with Abu Dhabi and Dubai. Once that had occurred, the Rulers of nearby Bahrain and Qatar would then be invited "to discuss together the future of the area and agreement with them on unified action to guarantee this." It is worth noting that, at least as it was written, the Union Accord did not necessarily contemplate the actual *participation* of Bahrain and Qatar as members of the union itself, even though Sheikh Zayed and Sheikh Rashid attempted to downplay the significance of this distinction in an additional statement issued two days later.

Regardless of the wording of the original agreement, just one week later, on February 25, 1968, the Rulers of Abu Dhabi, Dubai, Bahrain, Qatar, Sharjah, Ras Al Khaimah, Fujairah, Umm Al Quwain and Ajman gathered in Dubai in an optimistic attempt to seize the moment and create a much larger union involving all nine of them. Sheikh Zayed was skeptical that the time was right for such an ambitious step, preferring to focus on unifying the seven Trucial States in the first instance, just as the Union Accord had stipulated. He does not appear to have been opposed to the idea of a nine-member union in principle, but with the British withdrawal less than four years away, his instinct was to start with something smaller and grow from there. However, reluctant to be accused of disunity or to undermine Abu Dhabi's relations with some of its nearest neighbors, Sheikh Zayed agreed to throw his support behind the audacious plan nonetheless.

There were good reasons to doubt the feasibility of a nine-member union. Although the Rulers of the seven contiguous emirates were used to meeting together regularly under the auspices of the Trucial States Council, the nine Rulers of the Gulf had not met together as a group for more than three years. The involvement of Bahrain in the union also risked incurring the wrath of Iran, which at the time still claimed sovereignty over the small archipelago.

Despite these obstacles, the project appeared to get off to a blistering start. After just two days of talks, the nine Rulers proclaimed to the world that they had successfully reached an agreement to create a new federation, to be known as the Union of Arab Emirates, that would come into effect just over a month later on March 30, 1968.

Even in the glow of this diplomatic triumph, Sheikh Zayed remained unconvinced. Speaking to British officials shortly after the deal had been announced, he privately described the nine-member union plans as "*mufakkak*" (disjointed), and made it clear that, at least in his opinion, the wider agreement would have no effect on the recent union between Abu Dhabi and Dubai ("Since he and Rashid had made the union only they could break it"). On the contrary, his main priority was to expand the Abu Dhabi-Dubai union to include other members of the Trucial States, and by the end of March 1968, the Rulers of at least three of the northern emirates had expressed varying degrees of interest in joining it, up to and including putting pen to paper to that effect.

In October 1968, Sheikh Zayed gave a revealing interview to a British newspaper in which he publicly floated the possibility of a smaller federation involving just seven emirates, or potentially even less than that, being where things ended up. "No one can persuade us that there is some magic number of Emirates that placed together make a Union," Sheikh Zayed was quoted as saying. "We will not accept pressure as to numbers. Neither will any other

Emirate. My own view has been that even if two Emirates make a Federation that would be good. Such a two would then provide justification for others to join later."

Even as he kept his options open, Sheikh Zayed was an active participant in the nine-member union talks. In the view of one British official who knew the Ruler well, he was simply driving multiple horses with a view to potentially bringing them together at a later date. Presumably he was also open to the possibility of choosing the one that appeared to have the most stamina. At a dinner hosted on the sidelines of the second meeting of the nine Rulers, held in Abu Dhabi in July 1968, Sheikh Zayed gamely attempted to project a film documenting the group's triumphant first meeting using a tablecloth as a makeshift outdoor screen, but the backdrop flapped so much in the wind that the screening had to be canceled. It could have been a metaphor for the entire project.

In reality, the nine emirates were never really on the same page, with Bahrain consistently objecting to the proposed method for allocating seats in the planned national assembly or parliament, and Qatar appearing to favor a looser confederation than the kind of union that Sheikh Zayed and several others had in mind. Unable to reach agreement on many of the key constitutional questions that they had glossed over in their initial meeting, the collective enthusiasm for the project slowly evaporated. The nine Rulers would have their last meeting on the subject in October 1969, and the communique coming out of that gathering would never be signed. Efforts to revive the project would technically continue for another eighteen months, but the nine-member union appears to have been effectively over by the middle of 1970, even though nobody was prepared to admit it.

As the nine-member union talks drifted off course, Sheikh Zayed's life did not stand still. Throughout this period, he continued to oversee the running of Abu Dhabi and the long-overdue development of the emirate. He took a personal interest in the planning of Abu Dhabi City, including famously sketching his ideas for roads and other urban design features into the sand with his camel stick in order to convey the specifics of his vision to town planners and architects, including his desire for straight roads, public parks and ample green space.

A central pillar of Sheikh Zayed's planning philosophy was the need to ensure that family and tribal connections were respected and preserved during this period of dramatic urban and social change. Among other things, this meant devising housing and land use policies that would allow members of extended families to live in close proximity to one another in a manner consistent with their cultural traditions, even in the emerging downtown areas of Abu Dhabi City. Further out of town, it led to the creation of decentralized villages in which the members of Bedouin tribes and other rural dwellers could also gain access to modern housing and other amenities, such as electricity, schools and hospitals, without completely abandoning their traditional lifestyle, their ancestral ties to the desert, and in many cases, their livestock. Recognizing that the mere provision of facilities was not necessarily enough to ensure their use, Sheikh Zayed also began paying monthly financial stipends and offering transport to encourage more families to send their children to the emirate's new schools.

In 1969, Sheikh Zayed surprised many foreign observers by inviting Sheikh Shakhbut, his eldest brother and the exiled former Ruler, to return to live in the emirate of Abu Dhabi with his blessing. In fact, he personally went to the airport to welcome him home. Two days after he had first become Ruler, a visitor to Sheikh Zayed's *majlis* had boldly asked him whether Sheikh Shakhbut would ever be allowed to return to Abu Dhabi. Sheikh Zayed had replied that he hoped to invite his brother back in three years. At the time, British officials overhearing this had dismissed it as "[a] remark designed for public consumption," but it turned out that Sheikh Zayed had meant it. Just one year after Sheikh Shakhbut's return, in October 1970, the two brothers experienced the sad loss of their mother and the grand matriarch of Abu Dhabi, Sheikha Salama, who passed away with the knowledge that her sons had reconciled and remained true to the pledge that they had made to her as children to never use violence against one another.

In June 1970, the election of a conservative government in the UK raised hopes among some of the Gulf Rulers that the British withdrawal from the region might be reversed or delayed, giving them more runway to work with in their efforts to form a union. However, these hopes would be short-lived, and in early 1971, it was confirmed that the withdrawal of British forces would proceed as planned after all, and the longstanding treaties between the UK and the Trucial States (as well as Bahrain and Qatar) would indeed be rescinded by the end of the year. The emirates now had less than twelve months to prepare for their own independence, and they still did not have a plan for what would come next.

The relationship between Sheikh Zayed and Sheikh Rashid was tested once again during this period, casting doubt on the future of the Abu Dhabi-Dubai union. However, even though their tactical instincts were not always aligned, the foundations of the Union Accord proved strong enough to hold. The quiet divergence between the two Rulers around this time appears to have been caused by a genuine difference of opinion, with Sheikh Rashid believing that the best course of action was to begin with a looser union that involved as many members as possible that could potentially become more closely integrated over time (ie. start with something *simpler but larger* as a first step), and Sheikh Zayed favoring a more closely integrated federation with seven or less members in the first instance, that could potentially grow in size over time (i.e. start with something *smaller but more deeply integrated* as a first step). They eventually ended up somewhere in the middle (i.e. a seven-member constitutional federation that was closely integrated on paper, but in which the individual emirates still retained significant control over their internal affairs in practice). This would lead to some constitutional ambiguities at times, but it is also one of the key factors that has enabled the individual emirates to develop and maintain such distinctive characters over the years.

However, one year out from the British withdrawal, a workable solution of any kind seemed unlikely. Describing the state of play on January 1, 1971, just months before the establishment of the UAE, one senior British official wrote dismissively that in his view, Sheikh Zayed was "neither intelligent nor tough enough to see any of his bright ideas for compromise through to a conclusion." In an assessment that didn't age well, the same official added that it was "difficult to see Zaid as the leader of a federation of the Trucial States." He would go on to serve in precisely such a position for the next three decades.

Eventually, Sheikh Zayed decided that he could wait no longer. In a burst of executive action on July 1, 1971, he announced – in a radio address delivered on his behalf by his eldest son, Sheikh Khalifa, then Crown Prince of Abu Dhabi – the formation of a new Council of Ministers for Abu Dhabi and the establishment of a fifty-member National Consultative Committee that would advise the government on the running of the emirate's affairs. The reforms, combined with the sustained investment that Sheikh Zayed had made in the development of the now almost ten-thousand-strong Abu Dhabi Defence Force in recent years, sent a clear message to Abu Dhabi's neighbors that the largest and wealthiest of the Trucial States was prepared to go it alone if necessary, and could very well be on the brink of doing so.

However, Sheikh Zayed had still not given up on the idea of a federation. On the contrary, he was determined to give it one last shot. Less than two weeks later, in a dramatic meeting with the other six Trucial State Rulers, Sheikh Zayed drew a line in the sand and declared that the time had come for each of them to decide if they were serious about unification or not. One by one, the Rulers indicated that they were, but disagreements remained over the precise shape that such a union should take, with some favoring the conversion of the existing Trucial States Council into a quasi-governing body, and others – including Sheikh Zayed – insisting on the creation of something entirely new, more along the lines of the kind of fully-fledged federation that had always been beyond the reach of the union of nine. These differences of opinion are often whitewashed out of the official histories that are written of this period, which is unfortunate, because it diminishes the Rulers' achievement in overcoming these obstacles, both before and especially after the formation of the union.

It would take another week of negotiations, but on July 18, 1971, the Rulers of Abu Dhabi, Dubai, Sharjah, Ajman, Umm Al Quwain and Fujairah announced that they had finally reached an agreement to form a union amongst themselves, with Ras Al Khaimah staying out for the time being, ostensibly due to objections over the allocation of seats in the national assembly (now known as the Federal National Council). To be known as the United Arab Emirates (UAE), the federation would come into being on December 2, 1971, one day after the emirates' individual treaties with the UK were set to end. Bahrain, which had recently indicated that it planned to declare independence on its own, and Qatar, which was preparing to do the same, would not be involved.

Three years and five months after Sheikh Zayed and Sheikh Rashid had established the original Union Accord between Abu Dhabi and Dubai, an independent federation of the former Trucial States was finally coming together precisely as that agreement had anticipated, in friendly consultation with its neighbors in Bahrain and Qatar. Although the nine-member union had failed to materialize, the wider negotiations had not been a total waste of time. The provisional constitution that the six Rulers agreed to that day was a modified version of one of the earlier drafts that had been prepared for the abandoned nine-member federation. It is unclear whether the Trucial State Rulers would have produced such a durable founding document without the push-and-pull that the involvement of Bahrain and Qatar had injected into these earlier proceedings.

The provisional constitution created the federal system of government that the United Arab Emirates still has today. The highest body in the land, consisting of the Rulers of the emirates, is the Supreme Council of the Union (also known as the Supreme Council of Rulers or the Federal Supreme

Council). The President and Vice President are elected by and from that body, and serve renewable five-year terms. Decisions by the Supreme Council of Rulers require majority support, but on certain matters, that majority must include the Rulers of both Abu Dhabi and Dubai.

Beneath the Supreme Council of the Union, the system of government in the UAE also includes a Council of Ministers (effectively a cabinet), headed by the Prime Minister, and a National Assembly (now known as the Federal National Council or FNC) that includes representatives from all emirates. The allocation of seats in the National Assembly had been a consistent sticking point during the union negotiations. Under the provisional constitution of the UAE, Abu Dhabi and Dubai were given eight seats each in the FNC, Sharjah was given six, and Ajman, Umm Al Quwain and Fujairah were given four seats each. When it eventually joined the union, Ras Al Khaimah would be given six seats in the FNC.

The UAE would have its own flag, emblem and national anthem, but the red and white flag of each individual emirate – which could be traced back to the original maritime treaty of 1820, which required seafaring vessels from the Trucial States to display red and white flags as a way to identify themselves and signal their peaceful intent to British ships – could still be displayed within its own territory for the time being. The individual emirates would retain powers in a wide range of areas, including the right to maintain their own defense forces, and the natural resources and wealth of each emirate would remain its own property. According to the provisional constitution, Abu Dhabi would serve as the interim capital of the new federation for up to seven years until a new capital city, named Al Karama, could be built close to the border between Abu Dhabi and Dubai.

Following the signing of the provisional constitution, Sheikh Zayed – the putative leader of the imminent federation – set off on a whirlwind tour of the emirates that included stops in Dubai, Sharjah, Ajman, Umm Al Quwain and Fujairah. In cities and towns across the emirates, thousands of people lined the streets to celebrate the union agreement and to catch a passing glimpse of their future president. Their enthusiasm was vindicated almost immediately, as Sheikh Zayed announced a series of transformative water and electricity projects that demonstrated the tangible benefits that would come from membership of the new federation. These tours would eventually become a regular feature of Sheikh Zayed's presidency, allowing him to meet directly with people throughout the country to listen to their concerns and understand their needs and priorities.

"Any Emirate with three schools today is going to have forty schools tomorrow," Sheikh Zayed said, when asked how long it would take for people to see the benefits of unification. "The Emirate with no roads is going to have many. The Emirate with no hospital is to have both hospitals and clinics. The Emirate with no electricity is to have electricity . . . I believe that the reasonable man may discover the advantages for himself even after six months . . . He will then recognize how big this building of ours is going to be."

On August 15, 1971, Bahrain declared independence. Qatar did the same just over two weeks later. The UAE was next in line, but one major issue remained unresolved. Throughout the union talks, Iran had continued to assert its claims to one island under the jurisdiction of Sharjah (Abu Musa) and two islands under the jurisdiction of Ras Al Khaimah (Greater Tunbs and Lesser Tunbs), including objecting to the formation of the UAE until the issue of the islands had been resolved. In one conversation with British officials, the Shah of Iran indicated that reaching a settlement over the islands was a "*sine qua non* [ie. an essential condition] for wholehearted Iranian support for a Union." He had separately made no secret of the fact that, in the absence of a negotiated settlement over the islands, Iran fully intended to seize them by force prior to the withdrawal of British forces from the Gulf.

Aware that the UK Government had no desire to become embroiled in an armed conflict when it already had one foot out the door, Iran continued to pressure British officials and the Rulers of Sharjah and Ras Al Khaimah over the islands. As the deadline for the British withdrawal approached, the Ruler of Sharjah finally relented and reached a last-minute agreement with Iran over Abu Musa. Under the deal, Iranian forces would be allowed to establish a presence on a specific section of the island, and an agreed portion of any oil revenues generated from the island would be split between Sharjah and Iran. The Ruler of Ras Al Khaimah refused to strike a similar deal, but on November 30, 1971, Iranian forces occupied the islands of Greater Tunbs and Lesser Tunbs anyway, killing one Ras Al Khaimah policeman in the process, and sparking a diplomatic dispute that remains unresolved to this day.

Contrary to its longstanding treaty obligations, which technically still applied on the day of the seizure, the UK Government took no action to defend the islands. Despite reaching a negotiated settlement with Iran in advance, Sharjah's leaders did not fare much better than their neighbors in Ras Al Khaimah. After landing its forces on the section of Abu Musa specified in the agreement, the Government of Iran proceeded to claim sovereignty over the entire island anyway. The controversial deal also produced a backlash at home, and within forty-eight hours, four shots had been fired at the Deputy Ruler of Sharjah, who was hit in the chest and only narrowly survived the attack.

On December 1, 1971, the outgoing British Political Resident formally terminated the individual treaties between the UK Government and each of the Trucial States. The following day, on December 2, 1971, five of the Rulers, along with the Crown Prince and future Ruler of Umm Al Quwain who represented the emirate that day, met at Sheikh Rashid's guest palace in Dubai to reaffirm their commitment to the provisional constitution and to proclaim the establishment of the United Arab Emirates. At that moment, the gathering seamlessly transitioned into the first ever meeting of the Federal Supreme Council. Consistent with their powers under the provisional constitution, the Rulers elected Sheikh Zayed to serve as the founding President and Sheikh Rashid to serve as the founding Vice President of the UAE, and both immediately took their oaths of office. Sheikh Rashid's son and the Crown Prince of Dubai, Sheikh Maktoum bin Rashid Al Maktoum, was named as the UAE's first Prime Minister.

At noon, Sheikh Zayed led his fellow Rulers outside, where the national flag of the UAE was raised for the first time. Hours later, with the echoes of the twenty-one-gun salute from earlier in the day still ringing in his ears, Sheikh Zayed signed a Treaty of Friendship between the UAE and the UK. In addition to announcing the establishment of the UAE, the official statement that the six Rulers issued that day also condemned the Iranian seizure of the three islands, and left the door open for Ras Al Khaimah to rethink its decision to remain outside of the federation. Within a week, the UAE had joined the Arab League and the United Nations, and on February 10, 1972, Ras Al Khaimah would officially join the UAE, completing the seven-member union that exists today.

To most international observers at the time, the establishment of the UAE was either a bold political experiment or a naive idea that was destined to fail. Sheikh Zayed saw things differently. To him, the practical outcome of unification was to bring about a world that was closer in some ways to the one that he and other members of his generation had grown up in, before the search for oil had led to the emirates being divided by lines drawn on a map.

"Division is not natural to our people," explained Sheikh Zayed, reflecting on the history of the overlapping tribal lands that had been brought together to form the UAE. "In saying this, we are not speaking emotionally. It is an objective assessment. The concept of borders has never meant anything to our people, who used to move about the provinces of our land without asking, 'To whom does this area belong?' The land was his land, and that was strengthened by his sense of belonging to one essential group of people. In many cases, the individuals of one family would be spread across more than one Emirate. From this interweaving has sprung a very important fact: that we were united, then we were dispersed."

Now, the people of the emirates had been united again, this time under a single flag. It was a compelling theory, but it overlooked one important detail. As Sheikh Zayed and his fellow Rulers were soon to discover, even if the people were no longer dispersed, the lines on the map were still there.

NINE

Union in Practice

As the UAE's first President, Sheikh Zayed navigates a series of obstacles to the success of the new federation. Divisions emerge between the Rulers over the pace of federal integration. On the brink of a potential constitutional crisis, Sheikh Zayed and Sheikh Rashid reach a historic compromise to secure the long-term future of the union.

Sheikh Zayed hit the ground running as the founding President of the UAE. Although he was in uncharted political waters, the nature of the challenge was not entirely new to him, as he had been in a similar position just five years earlier when he had taken over the running of Abu Dhabi. The difference on this occasion was that he had just taken the controls of a government that did not yet exist. It was the political equivalent of building a plane while flying it. The good news, and the bad news, was that there was no model for how that needed to be done.

In his first few weeks in federal office, Sheikh Zayed signed a series of historic laws and decrees, including formally adopting the national flag of the UAE, founding the country's first national newspaper, and establishing the core functions of the Federal Government and bureaucracy. He also authorized the creation of a diplomatic service to represent the UAE abroad and negotiated the belated entry of Ras Al Khaimah into the union.

On December 22, 1971, Sheikh Zayed was granted control over the formerly British-led Trucial Oman Scouts, which were immediately converted into the first ever Union Defence Force (UDF). It would not be long before this new federal force would be called into action. On January 24, 1972, when the UAE was just fifty-three days old, the sitting Ruler of Sharjah, Sheikh Khalid bin Muhammad Al Qasimi, was killed in a failed coup attempt led by his predecessor, Sheikh Saqr bin Sultan Al Qasimi, who had been deposed seven years earlier, reportedly with British support. According to Sheikh Mohammed bin Rashid Al Maktoum, then the twenty-two-year-old UAE Minister of Defence, who reflected on these events in his book, *My Story*, Sheikh Zayed was adamant that the coup must not be allowed to succeed and instructed him to "resolve the matter quickly." The Sharjah-based UDF, along with members of the Abu Dhabi Defence Force, were jointly deployed to bring an end to the siege, and the leaders of the coup were eventually taken into custody.

While the dust was still settling on Sharjah Fort, the grieving ruling family chose the murdered Ruler's brother, Sheikh Dr. Sultan bin Muhammad Al Qasimi, to succeed him and to assume Sharjah's seat in the Supreme Council of Rulers. He would go on to rule Sharjah for more than fifty years. The coup had failed, but it was a timely reminder to all of the UAE Rulers that the ghosts of the former Trucial States had not been completely exorcized at the signing of the new constitution.

However, Sheikh Zayed and his fellow Rulers would have little time to reflect on these dramatic events. In early 1972, the country's leaders were consumed with the immediate task of rolling out basic infrastructure and services in areas such as education, health, housing, roads, water, electricity, agriculture, telecommunications and social security. In many places they were starting from scratch, with one of the Federal Government's first priorities being to provide electricity to every house in the country by the end of the decade. In its first three years, the UAE Government would pass fifty laws and issue forty-four resolutions and decrees, while staffing up its ministries and putting in place the necessary administrative infrastructure to deliver services across the country. A new national currency, the UAE dirham, was introduced in 1973, and citizens were soon issued with their first ever UAE passports, allowing them to travel abroad for the first time as Emiratis, rather than as citizens of their respective emirates.

Outlining the UAE Government's approach to foreign affairs in a 1972 speech, Sheikh Zayed said: "Our foreign policy sets four objectives: maintaining good relations and cooperation between the UAE and neighboring nations and settling disputes that may arise in the future by cordial, peaceful means; abiding by the UAE's commitment toward the Arab world and preliminary and fundamental Arab conventions; improving Islamic solidarity and cooperation with Muslim states in all spheres; and maintaining fruitful cooperation with all nations in all fields to establish security, peace and progress."

Having personally witnessed the economic devastation caused by the decline of the pearling industry followed by the Great Depression in his youth, Sheikh Zayed was determined to ensure that the UAE's economic future would not be dependent on a single commodity. "We must not rely on oil alone as our main source of national income," he argued, emphasizing the importance of economic diversification to the country's long-term security and resilience. "Indeed, we have to diversify the sources of our revenue and construct economic projects that will ensure a free, stable and dignified life for the people."

With that in mind, he prioritized the diversification of the national economy from the beginning of his first term in office through the development of agriculture, the growth of new industries and commercial enterprises, and sustained investment in education across the country. He also took decisive steps to begin investing Abu Dhabi's surplus revenues for the long-term benefit of current and future generations, beginning with the creation of the Financial Investments Board within the Abu Dhabi Department of Finance in the late 1960s (which eventually culminated in the establishment of the Abu Dhabi Investment Authority in 1976).

Under the dynamic leadership of Sheikh Rashid, the business-friendly emirate of Dubai would play a leading role in the diversification of the UAE economy and the growth of non-oil trade throughout this period, including through landmark projects such as Port Rashid (inaugurated in October 1971), Dubai Aluminium (est. 1975), Jebel Ali Port and Free Zone (opened in 1979 and 1980 respectively), Dubai Dry Docks (est. 1979), Dubai International Trade Centre (est. 1979 and now known as the Dubai World Trade Centre), Dubai International Airport (est. 1960) and eventually Emirates Airlines (est. 1985), the plans for many of which predated the establishment of the union. Building on the longstanding reputation of Dubai as a regional trading hub, there is no doubt that these groundbreaking projects helped to put the UAE on the global economic map in the early years of the new federation.

Ultimately, however, the UAE's most senior leaders were in agreement that the most important drivers of the nation's long-term economic success would be the Emirati people themselves, with Sheikh Zayed saying: "Whatever buildings, installations, schools or hospitals we erect, and whatever bridges or things of beauty we build, they are essentially material with no spirit. They are not capable of carrying us forward. The spirit that can carry us forward is in the individual who, through his thinking, his expertise and his ability, can maintain all those structures and go forward and grow with them."

Despite these early signs of progress, it quickly became apparent that a number of barriers were standing in the way of the successful growth of the new federation. First, there was an unsustainable amount of duplication between the responsibilities of the Federal Government and those of the local authorities, especially in the three largest emirates of Abu Dhabi, Dubai and Sharjah. Second, the UAE remained vulnerable to intimidation from its larger neighbors, including Iran, which continued to occupy the islands seized on the eve of the British withdrawal, but also Saudi Arabia, which refused to recognize the new federation until its border issues with Abu Dhabi were resolved, and which therefore continued to liaise directly with the Rulers of the individual emirates. It is hard to imagine now, but in the years after federation, there were still isolated armed clashes occurring on the disputed borders between the various emirates too, which was not exactly conducive to federal unity.

Perhaps more than anything, the political integration of the emirates was being hampered in the early years by the hesitation of some of the Rulers to cede certain powers and resources to the Federal Government, with Dubai in particular making no secret of its desire to maintain its administrative and commercial independence. In essence, this echoed the intellectual division that had opened up between Sheikh Zayed and Sheikh Rashid prior to the establishment of the UAE, and the competing visions that they had for how a federation of the former Trucial States should operate in practice. A compromise had been reached at the time and reflected in the provisional constitution, but their positions had never been fully reconciled.

Sheikh Zayed set about tackling each of these obstacles – the duplication, the intimidation and the hesitation – in parallel.

In 1973, in addition to playing a leading role in the oil embargo launched by OPEC members against the United States and others in response to their support for Israel in the fourth Arab-Israeli War, including making his widely-quoted declaration that "Arab oil is not dearer than Arab blood," Sheikh Zayed ordered the establishment of a high-level committee at home to examine the various challenges facing the fledgling UAE Government. When the committee recommended that many of Abu Dhabi's own government ministries should be dissolved, Sheikh Zayed led by example, and in December of that year, in his capacity as the Ruler of the emirate, he abolished the cabinet of Abu Dhabi headed by his eldest son, Sheikh Khalifa, and ordered the immediate transfer of a wide range of local government functions into the ministries of the Federal

Government. A new body known as the Abu Dhabi Executive Council was formed to oversee the local government departments and authorities that remained. These changes effectively dismantled the interim structure of government that the emirate of Abu Dhabi had hurriedly drawn up in July 1971, when it was unclear whether a federation of any kind was going to materialize.

Sheikh Zayed maintained that these kinds of adjustments were an inevitable part of the process, and did not reveal a flaw in the UAE's constitutional model. "There is no conflict between the federal and local ministries," he argued at the time. "However, duplication of effort may have occurred and that would be normal for such an experiment as ours. If there is any duplication of effort now, then the reason for it is that we moved so fast. We had to start somewhere; we had to deal with matters one by one. Mistakes may have taken place, but they were mistakes that took place through good intentions. With a desire to work, and with the passing of time, the State will stabilize, and such matters will be rectified. We have in fact seen this happening."

On August 21, 1974, after years of diplomatic outreach, Sheikh Zayed reached a historic agreement with the King of Saudi Arabia, known as the Treaty of Jeddah, which ended the long-running border dispute between Abu Dhabi and Saudi Arabia that had triggered the Buraimi Dispute two decades earlier. On this occasion, the matter was resolved without a shot being fired, and true to the King's word, Saudi Arabia immediately recognized the UAE as a sovereign state. Sheikh Zayed had entered the negotiations knowing that the establishment of strong relations between Abu Dhabi and Saudi Arabia would be crucial to the long-term security and stability of the UAE as a whole. Unfortunately for Sheikh Zayed, the Saudis knew that too, and when the terms of the Treaty of Jeddah were finally made public, it was revealed that Sheikh Zayed had given up a significant amount of Abu Dhabi territory in order to secure the deal, including rights to a valuable oil field. There was a sense of deja vu to these events, with the generous border concessions that Sheikh Zayed made to the King of Saudi Arabia echoing those that he had made to Sheikh Rashid six years earlier in order to facilitate the Union Accord between Abu Dhabi and Dubai. The UAE Government would later object to certain aspects of the Treaty of Jeddah, but its immediate effect in 1974 was to put the new federation on a far more secure footing in the region.

After resetting his relations with Saudi Arabia, Sheikh Zayed turned his attention to untangling the most sensitive set of obstacles standing in the way of the union: the hesitation of some of his fellow Rulers to fully empower the Federal Government. In 1975, the seven members of the Supreme Council of Rulers were handed a gloomy analysis prepared by the UAE Council of Ministers entitled, "Problems and Obstacles in the Way of Union." In the document, the Council of Ministers made a series of recommendations for strengthening the federation, including unifying the five separate armed forces that were still active in the UAE at the time, limiting the ability of the individual emirates to conduct their own foreign affairs, and initiating a process to make the UAE constitution permanent, rather than provisional, which left it subject to renewal every five years, and thus rendered its terms perpetually negotiable. In fact, the provisional constitution expressly envisaged its own replacement with a permanent constitution by the end of 1976. In its report, the Council of Ministers also pointed out that Abu Dhabi was still the only emirate making any meaningful contribution to the federal budget, even though it was no longer the only oil-producing state, and therefore called on others to begin channeling more of their own funds into the federal coffers.

Behind closed doors, the seven Rulers cautiously accepted a number of these recommendations, and a twenty-eight-member committee was formed to oversee the development of a permanent constitution. In November 1975, the Ruler of Sharjah – who had replaced his brother following the failed but fatal coup attempt of 1972 – proactively announced a sweeping series of actions designed to promote federal unity, including voluntarily ceasing the flying of the Sharjah flag, placing the Sharjah defense force under the authority of the Federal Government and, as Abu Dhabi had done two years earlier, transferring a number of local government functions to the most relevant federal ministries. By the end of the year, Sheikh

Zayed would proudly proclaim in a speech to the Federal National Council that the UAE flag was now flying exclusively across the country. However, Sheikh Rashid, in his capacity as the Ruler of Dubai, along with the Ruler of Ras Al Khaimah, both remained hesitant to relinquish greater control over their respective emirates' internal affairs to the Federal Government, at least at this stage.

Despite these differences of opinion, Sheikh Zayed continued to push for the strengthening of the federation. From his perspective, the pursuit of federal unity was not a sentimental ambition. It was an essential element for binding the nation and its people together. "The work of federating brings many new horizons," he said at the time. "The people must be satisfied that they have an interest in the federation, just as the businessman has an interest in his business, and the farmer has an interest in his field. How can a farmer be concerned about his planting if there is no harvest? The common benefits brought about by the federation are not just health, housing, education and standard of living; they are also manifest in the cooperation between tribes, clans and all citizens building a modern state."

On May 6, 1976, Sheikh Zayed announced the unification of the UAE Armed Forces under a single command. It is an event that is commemorated in the UAE to this day. Although at the time, the individual forces still retained a high degree of independence, the decision sent a clear signal that Sheikh Zayed was determined to pick up the pace of federal consolidation in the final months of his first five-year term as President. However, when the Supreme Council met again two months later to consider the introduction of a permanent constitution, the Rulers were unable to agree on its terms, and decided to renew the provisional constitution for another five years instead, against Sheikh Zayed's wishes. They also failed to resolve a number of outstanding issues related to immigration and defense policy, the financing of the federal budget and the settling of the lingering border disputes between the emirates.

There was no suggestion that Sheikh Zayed was losing the support of his fellow Rulers around this time. On the contrary, they were unanimous in their belief that he should be re-elected as UAE President. They just didn't share his urgency for adopting a permanent constitution and locking in terms that may not suit them in the future. Sheikh Zayed could not understand this. Five years into the federal experiment, he believed that the founders' original leap of faith had been vindicated, and the time had come for the Rulers to go all in. The details could be tweaked over time, but in such a formative period in the nation's history, the Federal Government needed to be strengthened and empowered, not reined in. Some of his fellow Rulers, most notably Sheikh Rashid, preferred to move more slowly in order to allow the UAE's federal system of government to evolve in its own time. As was so often the case between the two of them, their positions were not entirely at odds, but they also weren't remotely compatible. Something was going to have to give, and after taking some time to consider his options, Sheikh Zayed made a personal and political decision that took the entire country by surprise.

On August 1, 1976, Sheikh Zayed revealed in an interview with a Bahraini newspaper that he intended to step down and not accept a second term as UAE President when his current term ended in four months' time. As the Ruler of Abu Dhabi, he would continue to serve as a full member of the Federal Supreme Council, but the responsibility for leading the nation would fall to one of his fellow Rulers. He assured the UAE people that he would be "the first to back whatever president is chosen and the last to turn away from him," but the mantle of the presidency would no longer be his to carry.

The reaction to Sheikh Zayed's decision to refuse a second term as President was dramatic and immediate. The Rulers of the other six emirates, led by Sheikh Rashid, and an array of senior government officials from across the country, expressed their surprise at the news and their hope that Sheikh Zayed could be convinced to change his mind. That did not stop the Rulers from receiving a torrent of mail from their own constituents, urging them to resolve the issues that had led to Sheikh Zayed's decision to step down in the first place. The membership of the Federal National Council also issued a rare public statement pledging their allegiance to Sheikh Zayed and urging him to remain as President.

On August 6, 1976, which was the tenth anniversary of Sheikh Zayed's accession as the Ruler of Abu Dhabi, a crowd led by students from the recently established UAE University emerged on the streets of Al Ain to express their support for him. Similar rallies soon occurred across the country, with members of the public seen marching through the streets, displaying home-made banners and portraits of Sheikh Zayed. A petition began to circulate urging the President to accept a second term. A number of regional leaders, including King Khalid of Saudi Arabia, who had initially refused to recognize Sheikh Zayed's presidency, and Anwar Sadat of Egypt, also went on the record to express their hope that he would remain at the helm of the UAE for another five years.

On September 10, 1976, Sheikh Zayed issued a personal letter to the people of the UAE, thanking them for their support and welcoming their calls for federal unity. Twelve days later, he received a personal visit from Sheikh Rashid, who reiterated that all six of the other Rulers remained determined to find a way for Sheikh Zayed to continue as President. One week later, the first signs emerged that the die was not yet cast, when Sheikh Zayed publicly called on his supporters to cancel a demonstration that was planned to take place on the streets of Al Ain the following morning, in order to give him more time to discuss the challenges confronting the federation with his fellow Rulers. In reality, Sheikh Zayed had never fully closed the door on serving a second term. He just wasn't prepared to blindly accept responsibility for leading the nation unless certain conditions were met.

"I will give you an example," he said in a speech around this time, explaining how he thought about the dilemma that he was in. "If someone has a car which is not safe to drive, should the father of the family put his children in it being fully aware that it is unsafe? Of course not. The same goes for the ship which carries this whole nation; it cannot brave the sea with its storms and waves. Nevertheless, I brought this ship to harbor. I was responsible for its success in overcoming the dangers. Now, at the conclusion of my term in office, I am giving this opportunity to my brothers to take over. But, if the people insist and demand that I stay on and take on more responsibility, I could only accept with conditions and knowing that everything I need to ensure continued progress will be readily available."

This had been a longstanding part of Sheikh Zayed's leadership philosophy. Long before the establishment of the UAE, when Sheikh Shakhbut, then Ruler of Abu Dhabi, had asked his youngest brother if he aspired to be his deputy or perhaps even his eventual successor one day, Sheikh Zayed had apparently replied: "If my brother Shakhbut was Ruler I would like to be his deputy. I would then make a success of the job on behalf of everyone, provided I had *authority*. However, if I had no authority I would like to be a merchant. Yes, I would rather have nothing to do with government under such circumstances. Far better to go into trade!"

At the end of his first term as President, Sheikh Zayed got some, but not all, of what he wanted. On November 6, 1976, the Supreme Council of Rulers approved a number of amendments to the provisional constitution, most notably repealing Article 142, which gave the individual emirates the right to maintain their own armed forces. The President was also granted greater control over the sensitive portfolios of national security and immigration. With these amendments, and a renewed commitment from the Rulers to work towards the resolution of the other outstanding issues on their agenda, Sheikh Zayed agreed to serve a second term as President of the UAE. Accepting the appointment, he told the UAE people, "God be praised . . . I do not wish to relinquish my office until I have seen completed all the work we have undertaken, completed in the way we wanted. That is the way to make our people hold their heads high."

However, less than one year into Sheikh Zayed's second term, the fault lines began to reappear within the Supreme Council of Rulers, bringing the body's deliberations to a virtual standstill. In February 1978, these divisions erupted into view when Sheikh Rashid publicly objected to a major restructuring of the UAE Armed Forces that had been announced by Sheikh Zayed, and that included the appointment of one of the President's sons to a newly-created command position. Sheikh Rashid argued that the process had been unconstitutional, and most analyses of these events have concluded that he had a point. The changes were quickly reversed, but the controversy cast an ominous shadow over the relationship between the President and Vice President at a pivotal moment for the country.

Sheikh Zayed and Sheikh Rashid had been here before, of course, and in the aftermath of this latest dispute, they returned to the scene of their greatest compromise, and met face-to-face in Ghantoot, on the border between Abu Dhabi and Dubai – a short distance from where they had established the Union Accord eleven years earlier – in an attempt to resolve their latest differences over the powers of the Federal Government. However, no grand bargain was forthcoming on this occasion, with both men unwilling to compromise on anything but the most peripheral issues. At its core, their dispute was not unlike the question about 'the chicken or the egg,' with Sheikh Rashid consistently refusing to transfer more responsibilities to the Federal Government until it could demonstrate that it was capable of fulfilling them, and Sheikh Zayed arguing that the only way to build up the Federal Government's capabilities was to grant it more responsibilities.

In February 1979, just over two years into the UAE's second constitutional term, the Federal National Council and the Council of Ministers provided a joint memorandum to the Supreme Council of Rulers containing a new set of recommendations to strengthen federal unity and enhance the operations of the Federal Government. Their recommendations included specific measures to further accelerate the unification of the UAE Armed Forces and to expand the role of the Federal Government in a range of portfolios of national significance. They also proposed a new formula to determine the respective contributions that individual emirates should make to the federal budget.

One month later, on March 19, 1979, members of the Federal Supreme Council gathered in Abu Dhabi to discuss these recommendations. In what was becoming a familiar split at this point, the Rulers of Abu Dhabi, Shar-jah, Fujairah and Ajman were broadly in agreement with the proposals that had been put before them, but the Rulers of Dubai and Ras Al Khaimah were unconvinced that they were all necessary. As the Rulers attempted to break the stalemate, the familiar arguments being made inside the meeting room were soon overtaken by unprecedented events outside. In his book, *The Establishment of the United Arab Emirates 1950-85*, Abdullah Omran Taryam, who was serving as the UAE Minister of Education at the time, described the unlikely scene that unfolded on the streets of Abu Dhabi while the Rulers' meeting was taking place inside:

"Thousands of citizens from various walks of life, students, government officials and tribesmen, assembled in procession from various emirates and marched towards the place where the meeting was in progress. There they shouted slogans, calling upon the rulers to collaborate, demanding consolidation of the union, more powers for the federal institutions, support for the President of the state, and approval of the [FNC and Council of Ministers] memorandum."

Hearing the demonstrations gathering steam, Sheikh Zayed adjourned the meeting and went outside to address the people directly. He welcomed their commitment to federal unity, even though he did not endorse all of their ideas, and encouraged them to return to their jobs and homes, assuring them that he and the other Rulers had heard their message and were determined to address their concerns. Perhaps more than anyone, Sheikh Zayed was heartened to see this passion for the federation, which had only come into being as a political entity just over seven years earlier. More pro-unity rallies would be held across the country over the following week. "The unification measures called for by our people are proof of their awareness of what constitutes their welfare and an important indicator of their consciousness of the great benefits that unity will bring," Sheikh Zayed said at the time, interpreting the demonstrations as a raucous vote of confidence in the federal project. "Our people have tried 'Federation,' which is one form of unity, and have seen the tangible and positive results [that it brings]."

However, instead of returning to the negotiating table to hash out their differences, the Governments of Abu Dhabi and Dubai first resorted to trading contentious written statements in the local press. In the Arabic-language newspaper, *Al Ittihad*, the Government of Abu

Dhabi issued a detailed statement outlining its views on the future of the federation and decrying the refusal of the emirate of Dubai to transfer more responsibilities to the Federal Government. In response, the Government of Dubai published a defiant statement of its own in the *Dubai News* magazine, explaining its dissenting position. It was all relatively civil and lawyerly, but none of it was a good look for the country, and coming right on the heels of the Iranian Revolution, the sight of public demonstrations on the streets of a regional capital was enough to make the UAE's neighbors nervous.

Senior representatives of Kuwait and Saudi Arabia were soon sent in to mediate, and their joint intervention helped to bring an end to the dispute. By the conclusion of these discussions, a workable compromise had been reached, and Sheikh Zayed called for an end to the public demonstrations. For his part, Sheikh Rashid agreed to become Prime Minister of the UAE, in addition to his role as Vice President, where he would have a much greater stake in, and direct oversight of, the day-to-day operations of the Federal Government. It was a surprise move that stuck, and to this day, by historical convention, the sitting Ruler of Dubai serves as both the Vice President and Prime Minister of the UAE, where he oversees the work of the Council of Ministers. In March 1980, the Rulers of Abu Dhabi and Dubai both agreed to commit fifty percent of their respective oil income to the federation, making the UAE one of the most fiscally secure nations on earth.

"Is there any federated state in our era that does not face problems and disputes?" Sheikh Zayed would respond, when asked to explain the UAE's recent political challenges in an interview with an American newspaper. "So why is it strange if we too face problems and disputes, especially since we live in a tribal society with its own circumstances and peculiarities? Is not America one of the greatest countries in the world? It is federated and yet you also find fundamental disparities between the laws of its states. Those disparities do not affect the existence of its federated system . . . I am not saying that we shall be like America. But I am saying that if the main objective is the same, then the presence of a variety of points of view will not deflect us from achieving it. On the contrary, the existence of different points of view will give the work greater vitality and energy."

Almost two decades after these events, the UAE would finally get a permanent constitution in 1996, replacing the provisional one that had been adopted in 1971 and renewed four times since then. It was adopted unanimously and without objection. The most substantive changes to the text of the provisional constitution included the deletion of the word "temporary" wherever it appeared, and the official abandonment of the long-forgotten plans to build a new capital city on the border between Abu Dhabi and Dubai. It turned out that Sheikh Zayed, who had always believed in the wisdom of the original constitution, and Sheikh Rashid, who had always maintained that a clearer constitutional consensus would emerge among the Rulers over time, had both been right after all.

— TEN —
Summer Clouds

Sheikh Zayed strengthens the UAE's ties with its neighbors in the Gulf, culminating in the establishment of the Gulf Cooperation Council in 1981, but his wider goal of complete Arab unity is undermined by multiple wars in the region. The UAE Armed Forces participate in the liberation of Kuwait as part of Operation Desert Storm.

Sheikh Zayed entered the 1980s in an optimistic mood. The constitutional issues that had been hampering the federation since its inception had finally been resolved. The experienced and enterprising Sheikh Rashid had taken the reins of the Federal Government in his new capacity as Prime Minister. The various infrastructure and development projects that had been approved across the country in the last ten years were beginning to bear fruit.

In a bullish speech to the Federal National Council in 1980, Sheikh Zayed noted with pride that more than twelve thousand boys and girls had been enrolled in the country's primary schools in the last year. The UAE boasted one hospital bed for every 373 people and one doctor for every 918. Federal investments in electricity and water infrastructure had dramatically improved the quality of life of the local population, and the amount of arable land in the UAE had been increased by around nine percent in the previous twelve months alone. The UAE Government was in the process of conducting its first ever population census and a law had just been passed to establish a Central Bank. All in all, things were looking up for the burgeoning seven-member federation on the southeastern shore of the Gulf.

However, Sheikh Zayed's vision had never ended at the water's edge, and one of his first foreign policy priorities as President was the deepening of ties between the UAE and its neighbors in the Gulf region. Talks to expand regional cooperation had been ongoing since the early 1970s, and on May 25, 1981, a watershed moment was reached when the Gulf Cooperation Council (GCC) held its inaugural summit at the Intercontinental Hotel in Abu Dhabi, after being formed by the governments of the UAE, Saudi Arabia, Bahrain, Kuwait, Oman and Qatar.

As one of the principal architects of the new regional union, Sheikh Zayed was selected to serve as the first President of the GCC Supreme Council. He made no secret of the fact that he viewed the establishment of the GCC as an important milestone on the road to greater Arab unity, or as he put it, "the ideal example for global Arab cooperation, the driving force of the Arab League, [and] the crowning achievement of its Charter." He didn't know it yet, but the 1980s would turn out to be anything but unifying for the people and countries of the Arab World.

In an ominous sign of things to come, one of the first major challenges to be discussed by the GCC was the Iran-Iraq War, which had been triggered by the Iraqi invasion of Iran in September 1980. Following an emergency meeting convened in May 1982, the six GCC members issued a carefully-worded statement adopting a position of "strict neutrality" in the war and, at least publicly, spurning calls from Saddam Hussein for more emphatic Arab support. It was a controversial position to take at the time, and demonstrated that even the principle of Arab unity had limits.

Of course, strict neutrality did not mean total ambivalence, and Sheikh Zayed was outspoken in his condemnation of the conflict and the destabilizing effect that it was likely to have on the region as a whole. "This war does not profit anyone," he warned, urging both sides to rethink the damaging path that they were on. "Definitely not you, people of Iran, not you, Iraq, and not your neighbors. This is what you will realize when all of this is over. It is my duty to warn you. Shouldn't you think about the post-war period? All your dead and all the wealth you are sacrificing. Is it really worth it? This situation should stop and we are willing to contribute in order to put an end to it. Why think about war? Why not think about peace instead? If you are giving any thought to war, you should think even more about peace and the period that must follow the war."

The role of regional peacemaker came naturally to Sheikh Zayed, who by this point of his career had been resolving personal and tribal disputes on an almost daily basis for more than thirty years. Respected for his gravitas and diplomatic skill, the UAE President was called upon to act as a mediator in a series of disputes that flared up in the 1970s and 1980s, including between Egypt and Libya, Morocco and Algeria, among rival factions within Lebanon, and even between Somalia and Ethiopia. Sheikh Zayed's quiet diplomacy did not always succeed in bringing the various sides together, but he remained committed to the idea that the people of the region had an obligation to attempt to find a way to resolve their own differences without resorting to war.

This was a strategic judgment just as much as it was a moral one. One of Sheikh Zayed's primary concerns at the beginning of the 1980s was the prospect that a sustained period of regional instability could be used as a pretext for a stronger international presence in the energy-rich Gulf, including by the world's superpowers, which he suspected were determined to establish a strategic foothold in the area. After successfully navigating the treacherous waters that had confronted the UAE when it first emerged from the shelter of the British security umbrella in 1971 – and that many expected would scupper the union within its first few years – he now had no interest in simply replacing Her Majesty's Government with a different foreign guarantor just ten years later.

"The security of the Gulf is the responsibility of the countries of this region and their people," Sheikh Zayed asserted at the time. "Our concept of Gulf security is that the Gulf States are left to live in security and stability without recourse to foreign forces and without intervention by the major powers or others. This region is very important and indeed vital to the world and its economy. Perhaps the main factor that provides security for the Gulf region is that it remains remote from the superpower struggle."

At a press conference following the inaugural GCC Summit in Abu Dhabi in 1981, Sheikh Zayed indicated that regional leaders were united on this point. "The conference was decisive and binding with no split in it," he said, in relation to the prospect of foreign fleets and military facilities in the region. "The Gulf States do not need any foreign state or any foreign protection. That is to be ruled out ... There is no Arab or Gulf State that needs foreign countries to intervene in its affairs or to intervene for the purposes of protection."

He appears to have meant it. According to one Western media report, when former US President Gerald Ford – by that point working as a consultant for an American oil company – met privately with Sheikh Zayed in Abu Dhabi in March of the same year, he was bluntly advised behind closed doors that "the Emirates would never consider the question of allowing US bases on its soil." The depth of feeling on this issue at the time was at least partly due to Arab objections over the extent of US support for Israel, but the position was consistent with the wider policy of rejecting foreign intervention of any kind in the region.

Sheikh Zayed was not hostile to the major Western powers, but he was determined to set some clear boundaries in the UAE's relationships with them. "I have friendships and interests with the West but they are friendships that I myself chose," he explained. "No one can impose them on me. There is no friendship by coercion. I sell it my oil and I buy my goods from it. I give it the necessary facilities for commerce. I treat the West as the best and most excellent friend. However, setting up bases in my land and coming back to colonize me is something I just cannot accept or tolerate. When I need [help], I will ask for it. If it were a friend, it would come to help me. However, setting up bases in my land is utterly unacceptable. Otherwise, what is the point of all the weapons we bought, [and] the armed forces we trained and armed?"

Meanwhile, the ongoing instability generated by the Iran-Iraq War was being compounded by other regional challenges, including the ongoing occupation of Palestine and civil wars in Lebanon and South Yemen. To make matters worse, a sustained drop in oil prices had blown a hole in the budgets of the region's energy producers, leading to an economic slowdown and the cancellation of a slew of projects. The UAE's federal budget was forty percent smaller in 1984 than it had been in 1981.

Speaking in 1988, Sheikh Zayed was sanguine about the scale of the crises that the UAE and the region had faced over the last eight years. "The road so far, and on towards the future, has been strewn with obstacles, but with the help of God and his grace, we have been able to surmount all difficulties, and the process towards a better life has gone ahead with steady steps," he said in a speech to the UAE's Federal National Council. "We are absolutely certain that the dissension from which the Arab Nation is suffering is no more than a summer cloud which will soon pass and the darkness will disappear, because the Arab Nation is a reality that has existed for centuries and will be nothing without unity and solidarity."

Consistent with this outlook, Sheikh Zayed had led a group of Gulf states to restore full diplomatic relations with Egypt in late 1987. Egypt, which remained one of the largest and most powerful countries in the region, had been suspended from the Arab League for unilaterally establishing relations with Israel in 1978. "Since Egypt is a part of the great Arab world and the Egyptian population is part of the great Arab Nation of which each part is life-less without the other members, there is no way for Arab and Islamic causes to triumph without the gathering of its potential and capacities, and the strengthening of Arab ranks in order to face the dangers that threaten the future and our common fortune," he explained. "Egypt, with its human and cultural potential, and international weight, is as important for the Arab Nation as the heart for the body."

To the relief of almost everybody, the Iran-Iraq War finally came to an end in August 1988. However, rather than ushering in a new era of peace and prosperity in the region, the relative calm of the post-war period would be short-lived. Within two years of the war ending, the Iraqi Government would be directly accusing its neighbors in the Gulf, including the UAE, of producing oil in excess of the amounts agreed by OPEC members. The Iraqi President, Saddam Hussein, is also believed to have objected to having to pay back loans that his country had received from Arab countries such as Kuwait and Saudi Arabia during its eight-year war with Iran. By the middle of 1990, Iraq had begun massing thousands of troops on its border with Kuwait, while controversially accusing its neighbor of illegally drilling into its oil reserves. The region and the world held its breath, unsure if Saddam Hussein was playing a dangerous game of brinkmanship, or if he really was prepared to do the unthinkable and invade a fellow Arab country.

On August 1, 1990, Sheikh Zayed traveled to Cairo to discuss the rising tensions in the region with Egyptian President, Hosni Mubarak. Together, they made a renewed call for peaceful dialogue and the removal of the remaining obstacles to Arab unity. On the same day, Sheikh Zayed returned to a familiar theme in an interview with an Arabic-language magazine, describing the latest threats and accusations to come out of Baghdad as "a summer cloud, a passing thing between brothers." Later that night, Saddam Hussein would set the region alight by ordering the invasion of Kuwait.

Within hours of the first troops crossing the border, the UN Security Council issued a resolution condemning the invasion and calling on Iraq to immediately and unconditionally withdraw its forces from Kuwait. As tens of thousands of refugees streamed out of the warzone, Sheikh Zayed declared that all Kuwaitis fleeing their own country would be provided with housing and healthcare in the UAE for the duration of the crisis. Meanwhile, a large contingent of American and British troops was soon being assembled in Saudi Arabia under the auspices of Operation Desert Shield, sparking demonstrations in a number of Arab capitals against the growing foreign military presence in the region.

On August 10, 1990, Arab leaders gathered in Cairo for an emergency summit to discuss the unfolding crisis. Reports from inside the room described an unruly scene, in which the Iraqi delegates threw food at their Kuwaiti counterparts, and one foreign minister fainted. Despite the drama, the assembled leaders managed to approve a seven-point resolution proposed by the GCC countries that, among other things, condemned the Iraqi invasion and called on Arab countries to deploy their own forces to Saudi Arabia to help defend it from potential invasion and prepare for an international counter-assault.

The leaders in the room were anything but united, though, with the resolution garnering only twelve votes out of twenty-one, and a number of delegates voicing their misgivings about the apparent willingness of the Gulf States to join forces with the United States against a fellow Arab country. For his part, Sheikh Zayed was unrepentant about accepting American support, and placed the blame squarely at the feet of Saddam Hussein. "Is it our duty to save the face of the aggressor?" he asked. "No. He has got himself in this awkward situation and he must get himself out of it." In hindsight, Sheikh Zayed's response to these events provided two important insights into his evolving foreign policy doctrine: Unity is desirable but is not always possible, and war should be avoided at all costs but is sometimes necessary.

Eleven days later, it was revealed that the UAE had given the United States formal permission to station forces and cargo aircraft on its territory as part of Operation Desert Shield, in preparation for a potential air campaign against Iraq. Within forty-eight hours, a village of air-conditioned trailers had been assembled along the flight line at Al Bateen airbase in Abu Dhabi, providing temporary housing to more than five hundred US personnel. Coming on the heels of a face-to-face meeting between Sheikh Zayed and the US Defense Secretary, Dick Cheney, who at that time was the most senior sitting US official to have ever visited the UAE, the announcement was described in Western media reports as a major shift in US-UAE relations and a "political watershed in Gulf attitudes to overt cooperation with the United States military." It was also interpreted as an act of solidarity with Saudi Arabia, which up to that point had borne the brunt of regional criticism for hosting US forces on its soil.

As the UAE prepared for war, the nation also found itself bidding a sad farewell to one of its most beloved founding fathers. Almost ten years earlier, in May 1981, less than two weeks before the GCC had been formed in Abu Dhabi, Sheikh Rashid had attended what would turn out to be his last official event as the Ruler of Dubai and the Vice President and Prime Minister of the UAE. It was subsequently reported that he had suffered a stroke and, despite showing some early signs of recovery and appearing in public on several occasions during the 1980s, his day-to-day governing responsibilities were effectively entrusted to his sons from that point on. The devastating loss of Sheikh Rashid's wife, Sheikha Latifa, in 1983, is believed to have further accelerated his decline and cemented his withdrawal from public life, even as he survived her for another seven years.

According to Sheikh Mohammed bin Rashid Al Maktoum, the third son of Sheikh Rashid and Sheikha Latifa, who would also go on to serve as the Ruler of Dubai and Vice President and Prime Minister of the UAE, "What made him happiest during the final days of his life was sitting by the window in his palace in Zabeel, looking out over Dubai." Sheikh Zayed would reportedly fly to Dubai by helicopter during this period in order to spend time sitting alongside Sheikh Rashid on his terrace. The two men had not always seen eye to eye, but they had never lost their respect or admiration for one another, and this would ultimately prove to be one of the most powerful aspects of their political legacy. In the measured way that they had handled their differences over the years, they showed the nation and the next generation of leaders in the UAE (in this case, their own sons) that disagreements do not have to descend into personal disrespect or political dissolution, and that compromise is an inevitable part of governing in a functioning federation.

Sheikh Rashid passed away peacefully on October 7, 1990. He was succeeded as the Ruler of Dubai and the Vice President and Prime Minister of the UAE by his eldest son, Sheikh Maktoum bin Rashid Al Maktoum. Consistent with Islamic custom, his funeral occurred the following day, on October 8, 1990. Thousands of mourners came out to pay their respects, and as the lead vehicle driven by Sheikh Rashid's second-eldest son, Sheikh Hamdan, carried the late Dubai Ruler to his final resting place, Sheikh Zayed followed in the next car.

Addressing the loss to the nation, Sheikh Zayed described the late Sheikh Rashid as a friend, a great man and a remarkable leader, and praised him for the indispensable roles that he had played in the development of modern Dubai and the founding of the UAE. He reportedly told Sheikh Rashid's sons after his funeral, "As Sheikh Rashid was my brother, may God be my witness I consider you my sons." Almost three decades later, in his own book, Sheikh Mohammed bin Rashid Al Maktoum would indeed describe Sheikh Zayed as his "second father."

Meanwhile, the flow of foreign troops and military hardware into the region continued. In November 1990, UN Security Council Resolution 678 was passed which gave Iraq until January 15, 1991, to withdraw its forces from Kuwait before being forced to do so. By that time, more than six hundred thousand American troops had been assembled in Saudi Arabia as part of a military coalition that now had the backing of more than thirty-five countries.

When Iraq failed to withdraw its forces, the US-led coalition launched Operation Desert Storm on January 16, 1991. Pilots from the UAE, alongside those of five other GCC states, participated in the devastating five-week air campaign against Iraq, before hundreds of Emirati ground troops operating as part of the GCC Peninsula Shield Force participated in the infamous "100-hour" ground campaign to liberate Kuwait that commenced on February 23, 1991. Six members of the UAE Armed Forces would lose their lives in the conflict. On February 28, 1991, Sheikh Zayed's third-eldest son and the future President of the UAE and Ruler of Abu Dhabi, General Sheikh Mohamed bin Zayed Al Nahyan, traveled to Kuwait to visit the UAE's troops on the ground there. Sheikh Zayed would follow on April 24, 1991, as part of a wider tour of the GCC states.

Operation Desert Storm would last for only forty-three days, but the war would have a lasting impact on the attitudes of the Gulf states to their collective defense and the importance of the US-led Western security umbrella. It was not the only factor, but there is no doubt that the period after the first Gulf War coincided with a significant expansion of the UAE's defense and security relationships with major Western powers such as the US, UK and France. Sheikh Zayed was still a fervent believer in the principle of Arab unity, but if the events of the previous decade had demonstrated anything, it was that even summer clouds can bring rain.

— ELEVEN —
People Perish, Work Endures

As the UAE celebrates its twentieth anniversary, Sheikh Zayed is determined to ensure that the country's children and young people remain connected to the culture and values of their ancestors. Guided by his Islamic faith and his own life experience, he places particular emphasis on the importance of work to the success of individuals and the nation.

On December 2, 1991, the UAE marked the twentieth anniversary of its founding in 1971. The country had changed a lot in those two decades, and its children and young people were now growing up in a world that was largely unrecognizable from the one in which their parents and grandparents had been raised. For Sheikh Zayed, in his capacity as President of the UAE, this presented a new set of opportunities and challenges, including the potential for the country's immense wealth and generous social policies to lead to idleness and complacency. From his perspective, the most effective way to inoculate the country against this threat was to immerse its young people in the stories, culture and values of their ancestors, who had endured great hardship prior to the discovery of oil and the subsequent development of the emirates.

Sheikh Zayed placed particular emphasis on the intrinsic value of work, saying: "Work is of great importance, and of great value in building both individuals and societies. The size of a salary is not a measure of the worth of an individual. What is important is an individual's sense of dignity and self-respect. It is my duty as the leader of the young people of this country to encourage them to work and to exert themselves in order to raise their own standards and to be of service to the country. The individual who is healthy and of a sound mind and body but who does not work commits a crime against himself and against society."

In his own youth, Sheikh Zayed had been raised with the same principles, even though the nature of life in Abu Dhabi had been very different at that time. Under the guidance of his teacher and mentor, Sayed Abdullah bin Ghanom, Sheikh Zayed's childhood education was based almost entirely on the Quran, which he would reportedly study at night in the Ruler's fort under the light of an olive oil lamp. He learned everything that he knew through the lens of Islam, and its teachings came to influence every aspect of his life. Rather than rebel against his religious upbringing, Sheikh Zayed appears to have embraced it from an early age, taking comfort in the mysterious combination of certainty and humility that it provided.

Sheikh Zayed's belief in the sanctity of work was clearly derived from his faith. "My philosophy in life is based on my conviction that everything is in the hands of God Almighty," he once explained. "That which a man does he should do out of faith in God, and he should do it seriously and diligently." As UAE President, Sheikh Zayed often ended his speeches to government audiences with a distinctly spiritual call to action: "Do work that God, His Prophet and the believers may see your deeds."

The teachings of Islam also shaped aspects of Sheikh Zayed's accessible leadership style, perhaps best demonstrated at his daily *majlis* and during his frequent tours around the country. "When a Ruler becomes conceited and isolates himself from his people, then he is finished from that moment on," he once told an assembled group of government officials. "Conceit is fatal. No matter how much a Ruler knows – no matter how much anyone knows for that matter – conceit excludes him from righteousness and keeps him away from the true path. Our Master Muhammed (may the blessings and peace of Allah be upon him) was the best of men and the best of prophets. He used to meet with the people and talk to them. Anybody could approach him where he used to sit and ask him whatever they wanted. As for us, we are mere humans, we are not prophets. So, why don't we open our doors to everyone and meet with all?"

For Sheikh Zayed, the social and economic development of Al Ain, Abu Dhabi and the UAE had been entirely consistent with his faith, and not a diversion from it. "Nothing in the Koran conflicts with progress," he argued. "[N]othing at all in Islam contradicts with the need for physical progress, modern trading methods or learning. In fact, to the contrary, it incites progress. The tenets of Islam seek development."

To accelerate this development, Sheikh Zayed had no qualms about drawing on the technology, labor and expertise of foreign workers and advisors, including people of other faiths, many of whom found an unexpected home in the emirates. "Islam in its true essence provides guidance," Sheikh Zayed said. "This does not mean that it quarrels with other religions. In fact, by its own stand, it puts other faiths in equally high respect. Because, you see, Islam believes we are all servants of God. We are all equal. We have all of us been created by God in his wisdom."

This had been his view for as long as anybody could remember. In 1960, Sheikh Zayed had welcomed the American Christian missionaries, Pat and Marian Kennedy, to Al Ain, where they established the legendary Oasis Hospital. Nine years later, he provided land in Al Ain for the establishment of a Catholic church, known as St Mary's, the opening of which he attended. It is easy to underestimate what a controversial decision this must have been at the time. In fact, it is understood that some members of the local community did object to the establishment of a Catholic church in their town, but Sheikh Zayed overrode their concerns. Maybe he thought that the benefits of welcoming Christians to the area outweighed the costs. Maybe he didn't think there was a cost. Perhaps he knew that electricity would soon transform Al Ain far more radically than a mild undercurrent of Christianity ever could. Half a century later, officials in the UAE would be working on plans for the construction of a landmark interfaith complex in Abu Dhabi housing a church, a mosque and a synagogue on a single site.

In 1989, Sheikh Zayed purchased Tittenhurst Park, the seventy-two-acre estate on which John Lennon had written and recorded the song *Imagine*, which lies just two miles from the UK's Ascot Racecourse. Eighteen years earlier, at the exact same time as *Imagine* was being recorded there in May 1971, Sheikh Zayed and his fellow Trucial State Rulers were immersed in the final negotiations over the establishment of the UAE. It is unknown if Sheikh Zayed ever heard *Imagine*, but it is reasonable to assume that he would have quibbled with some of its lyrics, and especially its prescription for a world with no countries, no religions and no possessions. In Sheikh Zayed's experience, these things were a bulwark against conflict and disorder, rather than their cause.

The acquisition of John Lennon's former home was not Sheikh Zayed's only brush with fame around this time.

On one occasion, when the former heavyweight champion, Muhammad Ali, mysteriously failed to turn up for a book promotion tour in London in September 1991, his frantic publishers eventually tracked him down in Abu Dhabi, where he was patiently awaiting an audience with Sheikh Zayed to seek his support for an Islamic school being built in Chicago. Sheikh Zayed was out of the country at the time, so Ali had decided to wait for him to return.

Despite his growing profile and the endless demands on his time, Sheikh Zayed's connection to the desert and his passion for the traditional pastimes of his youth remained unbroken during this period. "Man cannot discard his previous life," he was quoted as saying in response to a question about the relative simplicity of his lifestyle. "I await the first opportunity amid my heavy responsibilities to go to the most remote parts of the desert, such as Liwa, between Abu Dhabi and Al-Ain, where I live among the tribes and mix with them day and night. There, I feel great relaxation. In the center of the desert, I receive inspiration from its clear spirit."

In his foreword to the book, *Falconry as a Sport*, Sheikh Zayed espoused the social, spiritual and character-revealing aspects of participating in a hunting party, and the connection that this tradition provided to the wisdom and values of the past:

"A hunting expedition with falcons brings together a group of men, never more than sixty and never less than ten ... The group may include a king, a governor, a prince or a prominent merchant or, again, just an ordinary man who has a house and a family to support, but a love of sport, friendship and a desire for the chase brings them all together . . . Each one feels a sense of release and well-being in both body and soul . . . These hunting expeditions bring out people's real character and reveal their nobility, integrity and moral excellence on the one hand, and their shortcomings and lack of principle on the other . . . By following this sport we are, after all, induced to remember our genuine Arab traditions and to hold fast to our ancient virtues and moral code."

For a long time, Sheikh Zayed had harbored an ambition to create a landmark mosque in Abu Dhabi that could accommodate tens of thousands of worshippers at one time and serve as a beacon for the Islamic virtues of peace, tolerance and diversity. Construction commenced in 1996, and at the time of its completion in 2007, the Sheikh Zayed Grand Mosque was the third largest mosque in the world, only smaller than those at Mecca and Medina. Predominantly made of white marble, the mosque was designed to be a functioning house of worship that would also be open to the public, thereby breaking down some of the cultural barriers that existed between Muslims and non-Muslims. Not everybody interpreted this gesture in the same way. In 2013, the singer Rihanna would be asked to leave the mosque after posing for a series of suggestive photographs on the site.

Sheikh Zayed was a devout Muslim, but there is no evidence that he ever fell prey to the kinds of extremist ideologies and intolerant sub-cultures that can be found within all of the world's major religions. He was prayerful without being pious, spiritual without being sanctimonious, and he had little patience for those that used their own faith as a cudgel against others, or as a way to look down on them.

"Islam is a civilising religion that gives mankind dignity," Sheikh Zayed explained. "A Muslim is he who does not inflict evil upon others. Islam is a religion of tolerance and forgiveness and not of war . . . of dialogue and understanding. It is Islamic social justice which has asked every Muslim to respect the other. To treat every person, no matter what his creed or race, as a special soul is a mark of Islam. It is just that point, embodied in the humanitarian tenets of Islam, that makes us so proud of it."

It may have partly been this personal sense of pride in Islam that motivated Sheikh Zayed to become such a consistent and outspoken critic of religious extremism. Frequently putting his head above the parapet, he drew little distinction between those that preached hatred and intolerance, and those who committed acts of violence in Islam's name.

"In these times we see around us violent men who claim to talk on behalf of Islam," he observed. "Islam is far removed from their talk. If such people really wish for recognition from Muslims of the world, they should first heed the words of God and His Prophet. Regrettably, however, these people have nothing whatsoever that connects them to Islam. They are apostates and criminals. We see slaughtering of children and the innocent. They kill people, spill their blood and destroy their property, and then claim to be Muslims."

For Sheikh Zayed, Islam had been the invisible force behind his entire life's work: From delivering water to the people of Al Ain with his own hands in the 1940s, through to the unification of the emirates and the development of Abu Dhabi and the UAE in the second half of the twentieth century, as well as the steady stream of humanitarian and foreign aid projects that he funded in Islamic and non-Islamic countries around the world throughout his presidency, in parallel with his own philanthropic giving. He was often content, but rarely satisfied, and he never seemed to believe that his work was done.

"People perish, work endures," Sheikh Zayed once said, drawing a bright line between the lives we lead on earth and the legacies we leave behind. "Each one of us must fill his heart with conscientiousness; God watches every movement, every action, all the work that we do. Our belief in the Resurrection and Judgement produces a conviction that this life is only a field being cultivated for the life of the Hereafter. Whoever is righteous in the first life is guaranteed victory in the second."

By the middle of the 1990s, Sheikh Zayed must have been aware that the end of his own life was waiting for him somewhere over the horizon. In the first week of August 1996, three hundred thousand flags and five million light bulbs were strung up along the streets of Abu Dhabi to celebrate the thirtieth anniversary of his accession as the Ruler of the emirate in 1966. The following month, he traveled to the United States to undergo delicate spinal surgery in order to relieve debilitating pain in his neck. When he returned to Abu Dhabi six weeks later, twenty-five thousand people spontaneously lined the streets to welcome him home, and tens of thousands more traveled to the capital in the weeks that followed in order to express their support for him from outside his palace.

Not long afterwards, Sheikh Zayed's protocol staff reportedly introduced a new policy requiring visitors to his *majlis* to arrive in groups, in order to reduce the number of times that the aging UAE President would have to stand in order to welcome new entrants to the room. However, a more serious threat to Sheikh Zayed's health would emerge at the turn of the century, when medical tests revealed that his kidneys were failing.

On August 14, 2000, a reportedly frail and jaundiced-looking Sheikh Zayed arrived in the United States, accompanied by an entourage of family members and close advisors, to undergo a high-risk kidney transplant at the Cleveland Clinic hospital. The UAE President took up residence in a VIP suite on the seventh floor of the hospital, which was decorated with his own rugs to make it feel more like home. He filled the days leading up to his surgery with a combination of medical appointments, meetings, government work and Arabic television. On August 17, he received a call from President Bill Clinton, at that point in the final months of his own presidency, who briefed Sheikh Zayed on the outcomes of the recent Camp David Summit, which had ended without a major breakthrough.

In the exact same week in the middle of August 2000, Marwan al-Shehhi, an unknown twenty-two-year-old from the emirate of Ras Al Khaimah in the UAE, attracted little attention when he passed his private pilot's test at Huffman Aviation, a small flight school in Venice, Florida. Al-Shehhi had been a student there for the previous two months, paying for his accelerated flight training with funds wired to him from Dubai. One month later, he would update his immigration status in the United States, reporting that he planned to continue studying aviation in Florida until September 1, 2001. At 9:03 a.m. on September 11, 2001, al-Shehhi would pilot a hijacked Boeing 767-200 into the South Tower of the World Trade Center, seventeen minutes after another commercial airliner had been crashed into the North Tower.

It was early evening in Abu Dhabi, and Sheikh Zayed, now a year removed from his successful kidney transplant, was watching live on television when the second plane struck the South Tower, confirming the rising suspicion that the dramatic events unfolding in New York City were not an accident. The UAE President immediately summoned his advisors, unaware that two of the five hijackers onboard the second plane – and at least two other men involved in facilitating the attack from the ground – had been citizens of his own country, ostensibly acting in the name of his own religion. It was the antithesis of everything that Sheikh Zayed believed in, and its cacophonous impact would resonate over the final years of his life, and reverberate long after he was gone.

— TWELVE —
Al Karama

Sheikh Zayed calls for greater international cooperation to combat international terrorism in the wake of the September 11 attacks. After backing military action against Afghanistan in 2001, he opposes the 2003 invasion of Iraq. Acting in secret, he devises a controversial plan for Saddam Hussein to step down and go into exile that almost prevents the Iraq War.

Sheikh Zayed moved swiftly to condemn the September 11 attacks and the poisonous ideology that had inspired them. He expressed his condolences to the United States in a private cable and a subsequent phone call to President George W. Bush, and the UAE Government publicly condemned the attacks and called for the immediate creation of a coordinated international effort to eradicate terrorism. Authorities in the UAE also clamped down on the extremist threat at home, reportedly making around 1,800 arrests of individuals with suspected links to Al Qaeda.

In mid-September, Sheikh Zayed addressed the Heads of Government of NATO (North Atlantic Treaty Organization) and the leaders of China and Russia, and repeated the UAE's call for greater international cooperation in the field of counter-terrorism, stating: "The UAE clearly and unequivocally condemns the criminal acts that took place last week in New York and Washington, resulting in the deaths and injuries of thousands. There should be a direct move and a strong international alliance to eradicate terrorism, and all those who provide assistance to, or harbor it."

Consistent with that position, the UAE Government severed diplomatic relations with the Taliban regime in Afghanistan, which was believed to be harboring individuals involved in the September 11 attacks. Sheikh Zayed also endorsed the commencement of coalition military operations in Afghanistan in October 2001 under the banner of Operation Enduring Freedom, including surprising many observers by committing the UAE Armed Forces to participate in the campaign, making the UAE the first Arab country to do so. The war in Afghanistan would continue for twenty years. Prior to this, the UAE Armed Forces had been deployed internationally on four major occasions, as part of the Arab Deterrent Force in Lebanon in 1977, as part of the GCC Peninsula Shield force in

Kuwait in 1991, and on peacekeeping and humanitarian missions in both Somalia in 1992 and Kosovo in 1999.

However, as senior US officials overseeing the emerging 'war on terror' began to turn their gaze westwards to Iraq over the course of 2002, Sheikh Zayed was less convinced of the need for military action and justifiably concerned about the volatile forces that such a move could unleash in the region.

On January 29, 2002, less than five months after the September 11 attacks, President Bush delivered his annual State of the Union address – widely remembered as the 'Axis of Evil' speech – on the floor of the US Congress, in which he indicated that, in addition to targeting terrorists and terrorist organizations directly, the US was now determined to actively prevent hostile regimes from acquiring weapons of mass destruction that could find their way into the hands of terrorists. Along with Iran and North Korea, the poster child of this state-based threat was Iraq.

In September 2002, President Bush ratcheted up the pressure in a combative address to the UN General Assembly, where he issued the Iraqi leadership with a specific list of demands, and in the following month, he addressed the American people directly about the growing possibility of military action:

"Some citizens wonder, 'After 11 years of living with this problem, why do we need to confront it now?' And there's a reason. We have experienced the horror of September 11. We have seen that those who hate America are willing to crash airplanes into buildings full of innocent people. Our enemies would be no less willing, in fact they would be eager, to use biological or chemical or a nuclear weapon. Knowing these realities, America must not ignore the threat gathering against us. Facing clear evidence of peril, we cannot wait for the final proof, the smoking gun that could come in the form of a mushroom cloud ... I hope this will not require military action, but it may. And military conflict could be difficult. An Iraqi regime faced with its own demise may attempt cruel and desperate measures ... If we have to act, we will take every precaution that is possible. We will plan carefully. We will act with the full power of the United States military. We will act with allies at our side and we will prevail."

The bellicose rhetoric played well in large parts of the United States, but in Iraq, it may have had the perverse effect of encouraging Saddam Hussein to dig in his heels. After all, one of the biggest unanswered questions about the Iraq War is this: If Saddam Hussein did not have weapons of mass destruction, then why did he continue to let the United States and the world believe that he did, when this all but guaranteed a war that he was bound to lose? Would a man really lead his own country to war just to save his own face?

Sheikh Zayed had always understood the powerful role that dignity (*al karama* in Arabic) played in human behavior. Throughout his life, in his dealings with people in many different situations, he had come to learn that human beings have a surprising capacity to act against their own best interests on principle, especially if they feel they are being disrespected. Nobody likes to be given an ultimatum, and from the *majlis*, to the dinner table, to the UN General Assembly, stripping another person of their dignity was rarely an effective way of persuading them to do anything.

This had been a consistent theme of Sheikh Zayed's. Decades earlier, when he was still serving as the Ruler's Representative in the Eastern Region of Abu Dhabi, he had reportedly urged his eldest brother and then Ruler of the emirate, Sheikh Shakhbut, to take a less confrontational approach with his own brothers, advising him: "If you want to make issue with one of your brothers, or want to blame them for something, don't blame them directly. Always try to use another of your brothers to approach in a friendly way the brother with whom you wish to take issue. Send a messenger. Make a bridge. But whatever you do, never blame directly or open your face to your brother in an aggressive way. If you do that, respect will inevitably be lost between you."

It wasn't always subtle, but sometimes that was the point. In the constitutional negotiations prior to the founding of the UAE, Sheikh Zayed agreed with his fellow Rulers that, rather than Abu Dhabi assuming the role of capital of the federation, a new capital city would be built halfway between Abu Dhabi and Dubai. It was a largely symbolic but important public concession to the other emirates that was, at least in part, intended to dispel the perception that oil-rich Abu Dhabi would seek to dominate the union. The name of this imaginary city that would be quietly erased from the UAE constitution twenty-five years later without ever being built? Al Karama.

Speaking to the writer Claud Morris in 1974, Sheikh Zayed outlined his approach to negotiating with others in the following terms: "It is of course easy to give an answer to any problems, big or small, and reach some kind of settlement. What is often difficult is to reach an agreement and keep your face and respect, and then move on to the future. To do this, of course, one must meet and understand people . . . All human beings have so many facets of character. If you do not understand the man with whom you are concerned it is terribly easy to place him in a position or a predicament he has never been equipped for, or created to handle . . . Yet if you truly understand a man and his origins you can bring him back to base, even help the man to understand himself."

By early 2003, it was clear that a number of the world's leaders had talked themselves into a precarious position over Iraq that they were not equipped to handle. Determined to prevent a costly and unpredictable war in the region, Sheikh Zayed made a determined effort behind the scenes to pull the world back from the brink, utilizing all of the lessons that he had learned from more than sixty years of personal, tribal and political diplomacy. His effort would ultimately fail, but the ailing Sheikh Zayed came closer to preventing the Iraq War than most people knew at the time.

On March 1, 2003, the Arab League held an emergency summit at a golf resort in the Egyptian city of Sharm El Sheikh to discuss the imminent US-led invasion of Iraq and its potential consequences for the region. Present that day were many of the Arab world's most powerful figures, including Hosni Mubarak of Egypt, Ali Al Saleh of Yemen, Bashar Al Assad of Syria, Muammar Gadaffi of Libya, and the future King Abdullah of Saudi Arabia. Sheikh Zayed was unable to travel to the emergency summit due to his health, but was represented on the ground by a high-level delegation led by Sheikh Maktoum bin Rashid Al Maktoum, then the Vice President and Prime Minister of the UAE.

During the opening session, a personal letter from Sheikh Zayed was distributed to the Arab leaders assembled in the room. The letter was unexpected and its contents were controversial. "Developments move very fast and bring with them huge and serious dangers to the Arab nation and the world because of the level the Iraqi crisis has reached," wrote Sheikh Zayed. "This crisis is getting complicated day by day and hour by hour, threatening to bring very serious danger not only to Iraq and its people, but on all of us and the whole world in general."

With that in mind, the UAE President went on to propose a detailed plan to prevent war in Iraq, based on the following four points:

1. The Iraqi leadership, including Saddam Hussein and his sons, would step down from their positions, leave Iraq within two weeks, and peacefully go into exile.
2. The Iraqi leadership would receive legal assurances that they would not be subject to legal action locally, regionally or internationally.
3. An amnesty would be issued protecting other Iraqis connected to the regime, both inside and outside the country, from legal action.
4. The Arab League, in cooperation with the United Nations, would supervise the situation in Iraq for a transitional period until self-governance could be restored.

Sheikh Zayed's letter was the first official call from a fellow Arab leader for Saddam Hussein to step down in order to avoid war, and it received a cool reception in Sharm El Sheikh. In fact, it was not even formally considered. According to media reports, Amr Moussa, then-Secretary General of the Arab League, refused to allow Sheikh Zayed's proposal to be debated at the summit for protocol reasons, ostensibly because it had not been submitted in advance to a meeting of Arab League foreign ministers held some weeks earlier. In other words, it had been sprung on the assembled leaders without notice.

However, according to UAE officials, unbeknownst to the Arab leaders in Sharm El Sheikh (including members of the Iraqi delegation who dismissed the proposal as "dirty psychological warfare played by the American administration"), the terms of the exile plan outlined in Sheikh Zayed's letter had been discussed, negotiated and agreed with Saddam Hussein himself, over the course of four secret meetings. One of his final conditions was Arab League approval of the deal. There is no guarantee that the volatile Saddam Hussein would have held up his end of the bargain, but the deal created a viable exit ramp, and UAE officials maintain that he was willing to take it. The US Government had also been aware of the secret negotiations and was reportedly open to the plan too. In theory, it could have been a way out for everyone.

"Our last-ditch hope was that Saddam would agree to go into exile," George W. Bush would later write in his memoir, describing the lead-up to the war in March 2003. "At one point, an offer from a Middle Eastern government to send Saddam to Belarus with $1 to $2 billion looked like it might gain traction. Instead, in one of his final acts, Saddam ordered the tongue of a dissident slashed out and left the man to bleed to death. The dictator of Iraq had made his decision. He chose war."

The exile plan contained all of the hallmarks of Sheikh Zayed's political philosophy. If there was a Zayed doctrine, you could argue that it consisted of the following four elements: Dignity, in terms of treating people with respect, even if you disagreed with them; patience, in terms of not taking dramatic action unless it was absolutely necessary; foresight, in terms of conducting due diligence to understand the likely consequences of a particular course of action before taking it; and unity, in terms of building consensus and operating in concert with others wherever possible.

By contrast, the actions of the US and UK Governments in the lead-up to the Iraq War ran counter to every one of these instincts. In 2016, the UK Government's own inquiry into the Iraq War would conclude, among other things, that the conflict was launched before all peaceful options had been exhausted, over the objections of a majority of UN Security Council members, and on the basis of flawed intelligence and an underestimation of the foreseeable consequences of the invasion.

In fairness, the Arab League did not exactly cover itself in glory in the lead-up to the Iraq War either. Rather than unify behind the only viable plan to avert the war, Arab leaders in Sharm El Sheikh issued a bland statement to condemn the imminent US-led invasion, but took no meaningful steps to prevent it. The summit effectively collapsed after a heated argument erupted between the leaders of Saudi Arabia and Libya that led to the broadcast feed being cut. Sheikh Zayed's exile plan lay on the table throughout the calamitous seven-hour meeting, condemned loudly by some, welcomed quietly by others, but otherwise ignored.

"The Arabs unfortunately didn't have the courage of discussing it in a proper forum," lamented Sheikh

Abdullah bin Zayed Al Nahyan, then the UAE Minister of Information and the future UAE Minister of Foreign Affairs, who described his father's exile plan as "the last hope of an Arab solution."

Reflecting on these events two years later, Sheikh Mohamed bin Zayed Al Nahyan, then Crown Prince of Abu Dhabi and Deputy Supreme Commander of the UAE Armed Forces, and the future President of the UAE, said:

"During those days, the circumstances we worked under needed a very swift decision, an immediate response. We had the final acceptance of the various parties . . . the main players in the world and the concerned person, Saddam Hussein. We were coming to place the facts on the table. The results would have emerged if the initiative was presented and discussed."

Writing in support of Sheikh Zayed's proposal in the Abu Dhabi-based *Al Ittihad* newspaper in the immediate aftermath of the emergency summit, Dr. Anwar Gargash, who would eventually go on to serve as the UAE Minister of State for Foreign Affairs, argued that the exile plan was motivated above all by concern for the Iraqi people, who were destined to bear the brunt of any US-led invasion. "Homelands are eternal, but presidents and leaders are transient," wrote Gargash. "The way out is clear: either Sheikh Zayed's initiative or lighting the fuse of war and destruction." An editorial in a major Saudi newspaper also lauded Sheikh Zayed for having the courage to put into words what many other Arab leaders were thinking but were not prepared to say. Other commentators questioned why the UAE would allow Sheikh Zayed's name to be associated with such a controversial proposal.

The exile plan did not completely die in Sharm El Sheikh. The following day, the UAE Government raised it again at the 86th GCC Foreign Ministers' meeting in Doha, Qatar, indicating that the proposal remained on the table. Leaders in Saudi Arabia, Kuwait and Bahrain eventually expressed their support for the plan, and the communique coming out of the GCC Foreign Ministers' meeting called for further discussion of the idea. However, the initiative failed to gather broader support and the fragile momentum behind it soon petered out.

Three weeks later, the US and its allies commenced military operations in Iraq. The Iraq War would rage for the better part of a decade, and the instability that it unleashed would have far-reaching and long-lasting consequences for the region and the world. Fifteen years after the invasion of Iraq, the decision to go to war was estimated to have led to the loss of more than five hundred thousand lives.

In 2008, five years after the war began, Amr Moussa, then still Secretary General of the Arab League, who had reportedly blocked discussion of the UAE's exile plan at the emergency summit in Sharm El Sheikh, said the following when reflecting on these events: "I totally agreed with Sheikh Zayed. He was right. Although the situation was quite complex and tricky, we could have avoided all that had we taken that decision and implemented it."

— THIRTEEN —
The Nation Mourns

Sheikh Zayed dies in Abu Dhabi on November 2, 2004. His passing leads to an outpouring of grief in the UAE and around the world. He is succeeded as the Ruler of Abu Dhabi and President of the UAE by his eldest son, Sheikh Khalifa bin Zayed Al Nahyan, who pledges that the UAE will continue to be guided by the legacy and values of the late Sheikh Zayed.

As 2003 began to draw to a close, the first public signs emerged that Sheikh Zayed was putting his personal and political affairs in order with a view to his eventual succession. By this point, he was around eighty-five years of age and, along with the Ruler of Ras Al Khaimah, he was one of the last two Rulers to remain out of the original seven that had come together to form the UAE three decades earlier.

On December 1, 2003, in his capacity as the Ruler of Abu Dhabi, Sheikh Zayed issued a decree appointing his third-eldest son, Sheikh Mohamed bin Zayed Al Nahyan, to the newly-created position of Deputy Crown Prince of Abu Dhabi. The decree left little room for ambiguity over its intent, by not just appointing Sheikh Mohamed to this new position, but by explicitly authorizing him to assume the role of Crown Prince of Abu Dhabi when it next became vacant.

The announcement was unprecedented but also unsurprising. Born in 1961, Sheikh Mohamed had served as the Chief of Staff of the UAE Armed Forces since 1993 and been promoted to the rank of Lieutenant General in 1994. A qualified pilot and a graduate of the UK's Sandhurst military academy, he had previously served as the commander of the UAE's Air Force and Air Defence. By the time of his appointment as Deputy Crown Prince of Abu Dhabi, he had served for years as Sheikh Zayed's chief advisor on national security issues and as an influential member of the economically significant Supreme Petroleum Council. He had been entrusted with overseeing the sensitive involvement of the UAE Armed Forces in Afghanistan and had long been known in international defense circles as a key figure in military decision-making in the UAE. In the immediate aftermath of the September 11 attacks, he had personally led the implementation of an audit of the UAE's own security vulnerabilities before taking a series of aggressive steps to disrupt terror finance networks and counter the influence of extremist ideology in the region. Now, at forty-two years of age, he was officially second in the line of succession to eventually serve as the Ruler of Abu Dhabi.

Accepting his appointment as Deputy Crown Prince, Sheikh Mohamed said: "In every position of responsibility I serve, I consider myself a soldier who fulfills the commands and directives of His Highness Sheikh Zayed bin Sultan Al Nahyan and His Highness Sheikh Khalifa bin Zayed Al Nahyan, Abu Dhabi Crown Prince and Deputy Supreme Commander of the Armed Forces."

The following day, on December 2, 2003, Sheikh Zayed delivered what would turn out to be his final address to the nation on the occasion of UAE National Day, which is celebrated each year on the anniversary of the country's founding in 1971. It is unclear whether Sheikh Zayed knew that this would be his final National Day address, but there are reasons to suspect that he may have had some idea.

He began in the traditional way, by expressing his pride in the country's achievements, including the involvement of the UAE Armed Forces in international peacekeeping and humanitarian efforts around the world, the impact of the country's foreign aid and development assistance programs, and its domestic progress in areas such as human development, emiratization and women's empowerment. Turning to foreign policy, he expressed the UAE's continuing solidarity with its neighbors in the Gulf, reiterated its commitment to supporting the people of war-torn Iraq, called on the international community to work towards the resolution of the Palestinian issue, and reaffirmed the UAE's claim to sovereignty over the three islands occupied by Iran on the eve of federation.

At its core, though, the address was not a victory lap. On the contrary, it was a sweeping call to action, and a declaration that perhaps only Sheikh Zayed could make, that the era of the founding fathers was coming to an end, and the country was entering a new phase in which more would be expected of its people, and especially its younger generations. It was also a clear-eyed warning that the future of the country was not guaranteed, just as its progress to date had not been inevitable:

> "My dear citizens, work for our nation does not cease – it is a never-ending task – and it is your responsibility, oh young men and women of the Emirates, to make the best use of the opportunities that have been given to you, in order to provide you with the means to contribute to your country and to your people. We view the concept of citizenship as meaning loyalty to our country and a commitment to work for its benefit. Citizenship requires from each and every one of us that we should view the making of a contribution to our country as the yardstick by which we are judged, because the homeland is a single entity, and the building of it necessitates that all of us should work together, hand in hand, and that all of us should be ready to serve and protect it.

The evidence of our material development that you see all around you did not emerge from nothing. It is the result of hard work, perseverance and commitment. What has come about did not happen all of a sudden, and nor did it just take place over the course of the last three or four decades. It is the result of the cultural and social heritage that we inherited from our fathers and our forefathers, who faced difficulties that are today beyond our capacity to imagine. We are indebted to them for all that we enjoy in terms of our strength, our ability to build, our seriousness in work and our determination to succeed. That is why we always say that a people that does not understand its past, and does not draw the correct lessons from it, will not be able to deal with the challenges of the present and the future.

We will continue with all of our capabilities, and at all official and non-official levels, to protect and to safeguard our achievements and accomplishments, so that we may do yet more for the good of our people and our country. But we now look for real participation in this task by all of you, both men and women, a participation that is effective in the process of development, with all of its vital economic, social and cultural dimensions.

Oh, young men and women of the Emirates, the future is yours. You are those who will determine its features. Make the best use of the opportunities that have been made available to you, and use them prudently and rationally, so as to benefit your families and your country . . .

What we have achieved, my dear young people of the Emirates, will not survive, unless you yourselves engage in further work and efforts, and sacrifices. You should work hard to protect our national achievements, to foster and support the continued march of our Federation, and to make more achievements that contribute to the dignity and prestige of our country and to the welfare of our people. This cannot be achieved without positive and effective participation from all of you.

Today, we enjoy a prosperity the likes of which we never even dreamed. I appeal to you all, young men and women of the Emirates, to do all that you can to preserve and to cherish it, so that you and your children may continue to enjoy its fruits. Spare no effort to work with all of your powers. I warn you against idleness, and against taking things easy. What we enjoy today will not stay as it is without hard work, and without the continued blessings of Almighty God. Please do not fail us. Oh, young men and women of the Emirates. Work for your country with devotion and sincerity. Engage in interaction with the world around you. Take from it what is useful to you and to your country, and leave aside those things that are harmful to your society, your traditions and your values."

These cautionary words are rarely cited in the UAE today, but Sheikh Zayed chose to put these things on the record for a reason, and they provide a telling window into what was on his mind in the final year of his life. Three decades earlier, at the founding of the nation in 1971, the UAE's first President had carried himself with unshakeable confidence and determination, his words and demeanor communicating to the people of the emirates that everything was going to work out, even if the odds were stacked against them. Now, in what would turn out to be his final National Day address, with the union richer and stronger than it had ever been before, he appeared to be doing the opposite, and leaving the people of the UAE with a solemn warning that, despite the country's many advantages, or perhaps because of them, a passive slide into comfort and complacency would be catastrophic.

Eleven months later, on November 1, 2004, it was announced via the Emirates News Agency that Sheikh Zayed had ordered a curious reshuffle of the UAE Cabinet, reportedly at the suggestion of Sheikh Maktoum bin Rashid Al Maktoum, the UAE Vice President and Prime Minister. This was only the seventh cabinet reshuffle since federation, and the changes included the historic appointment of the UAE's first female minister, the merger of a number of federal ministries, and the creation of a mysterious new entity known as the Ministry of Presidential Affairs, which would be headed by one of Sheikh Zayed's sons, Sheikh Mansour bin Zayed Al Nahyan.

The following day, on November 2, 2004, Sheikh Zayed passed away at Al Bateen Palace in Abu Dhabi. He was around eighty-six years of age. His death was announced in a melancholy statement that read: "The Presidential Court announces to the people of the Emirates, the Arab and Muslim worlds and the entire world that the leader of the nation and the builder of its civilization, His Highness Shaikh Zayed bin Sultan Al Nahyan, died on the evening of Tuesday, November 2, the 19th of Ramadan. May God have mercy on him."

The announcement led to an immediate outpouring of grief throughout the country. One local news anchor was famously brought to tears on air as he announced Sheikh Zayed's passing to the nation, and local television broadcasts were soon switched over to readings of the Quran.

It was declared that a national period of mourning would be observed for the next forty days, during which flags would be flown at half-mast throughout the UAE. Other Arab countries, and some non-Arab countries such as India and Pakistan, would soon declare their own three-day mourning periods. Both Syria and Yemen suspended their own television broadcasts and replaced them with Quranic readings. Even the President of Iran, which remained in a decades-long territorial dispute with the UAE, issued a personal condolence message expressing his sorrow at the death of Sheikh Zayed, who he described as a "sagacious leader who worked for global peace and stability, and vigorously pursued prosperity for his people."

Consistent with Islamic custom, Sheikh Zayed's funeral was held before sunset on the day following his death on November 3, 2004, at the Sultan bin Zayed Mosque, which had been named after his late father, in the

Al Bateen area of Abu Dhabi. As thousands of mourners gathered outside to pay their respects, the male family and friends of Sheikh Zayed, including his sons and grandsons, led by the grieving Sheikh Khalifa, accompanied by the Rulers and Crown Princes of the emirates, led by Sheikh Maktoum, solemnly gathered to perform the Islamic funeral prayer over the flag-draped body of the late UAE President. The ceremony was also attended by leaders and senior officials from a large number of Arab and Muslim countries who had traveled to Abu Dhabi in the previous twenty-four hours.

Following the Islamic funeral prayer, Sheikh Zayed's coffin was carried to a waiting vehicle to undertake the short journey to his final resting place on the grounds of the yet-to-be-completed Sheikh Zayed Grand Mosque. It was estimated that over one hundred thousand people lined the streets of Abu Dhabi as the funeral cortege, involving up to 150 vehicles, slowly made its way to the burial site, crossing through the intersection of Al Khaleej Al Arabi and Sa'ada Streets at 4:00 p.m. According to international news reports, some mourners reportedly threw themselves to the ground in anguish as the cortege passed by, while most stood in solemn silence. The late Sheikh Zayed was then finally laid to rest in a small burial plot in the shadows of the mosque that would carry his name.

As the Crown Prince of Abu Dhabi, Sheikh Khalifa had been anointed before his father's death as his rightful successor as the Ruler of the emirate. His younger brother,

Sheikh Mohamed, had been named as his successor as Crown Prince. However, the issue of succession was more complicated at the federal level, at least on paper. Although it was widely expected that Sheikh Khalifa would also succeed his father as the President of the UAE, it was not a foregone conclusion. The federal constitution stipulates that in the event of the death or resignation of the President, the Vice President can serve as the Acting President of the UAE for a period of up to thirty days until the Supreme Council of Rulers elects a permanent replacement.

In the end, it wouldn't take anywhere near that long. Less than four hours after Sheikh Zayed's funeral had taken place, the Rulers sat together at Al Bateen Palace in Abu Dhabi, where Sheikh Khalifa and his family were receiving condolences. According to Sheikh Sultan bin Mohammed Al Qasimi, the Ruler of Sharjah, in comments made to Al Arabiya television, the succession was worked out between the Rulers in less than ten minutes. In Sheikh Sultan's telling, Sheikh Maktoum asked him if it was really necessary to wait thirty days to appoint a new President. Sheikh Sultan clarified that, according to the constitution, the change had to occur *within* 30 days, not after it. "Why not do it now?", Sheikh Maktoum apparently replied.

The Rulers repaired to a room adjacent to the main *majlis*, where Sheikh Maktoum is believed to have informed Sheikh Khalifa of their unanimous desire for him to succeed his father as UAE President. Initially, Sheikh Khalifa is said to have demurred, purportedly out of deference to

Sheikh Maktoum's experience as the sitting Vice President. However, the six other Rulers insisted, and in their constitutional capacity as the Federal Supreme Council, a vote was held on the spot to elect Sheikh Khalifa as the new President of the UAE. The decision was announced to the public later that night.

It was expected that Sheikh Khalifa would receive condolences at Al Bateen Palace for three days, but this period would eventually have to be extended due to the number of visitors that wished to pay their respects. Her Highness Sheikha Fatima, wife of the late Sheikh Zayed, also received a steady stream of condolences from female mourners over the following week, including the wives of regional leaders and foreign ambassadors in the UAE.

Sheikh Zayed's broader impact outside of the Middle East became powerfully evident in the days after his death, as tributes flowed in from distant capitals. Obituaries published in newspapers around the world attempted to distill his personal story and political legacy into a few hundred words.

Kofi Annan, UN Secretary General, issued a statement expressing his "profound sadness" at the death of Sheikh Zayed, who he described as "a most distinguished statesman," whose "wisdom, strong belief in diplomacy and generous assistance to developing countries also won him wide renown outside his own country – in the Islamic world and even further afield."

US President George W. Bush, who was elected to a second term on the day that Sheikh Zayed died, said, "The United States mourns the passing of a great friend of our country, Sheikh Zayed bin Sultan Al Nahyan of the United Arab Emirates. Sheikh Zayed was the founder and President of the UAE for more than 30 years, a pioneer, an elder statesman, and a close ally. He and his fellow rulers of the seven Emirates built their federation into a prosperous, tolerant, and well-governed state."

French President, Jacques Chirac, who abandoned a European summit meeting to travel to Abu Dhabi in order to extend his condolences to Sheikh Khalifa in person, expressed his "deep sorrow and emotion" at the death of Sheikh Zayed, who he described as a personal friend and a "man of peace and vision, [who] kept promoting the virtues of compromise, reason and dialogue in a region troubled by crises and conflicts."

Her Majesty Queen Elizabeth said, "I am sure that the prosperity of the United Arab Emirates today will be widely seen as a testament to Sheikh Zayed's wisdom, skill and devotion to the service of the state."

The city of Amman, Jordan, named a street after Sheikh Zayed. According to one report, more than twenty Mauritanian babies were named "Zayed" in the five days after his death.

Shortly after Sheikh Zayed's passing, a reporter from a local newspaper interviewed two elders from the Manasir tribe living on the outskirts of Abu Dhabi City. The Manasir had been one of the most formidable Bedouin tribes in the desert areas around Al Ain when Sheikh Zayed had moved there as a child in the 1920s. It had also maintained a strong presence in the Liwa region, and its tribesmen, who were known for their "toughness and daring," had regularly fought alongside those of the Bani Yas in the fierce tribal battles of the not-so-distant past.

The two tribesmen recalled how, even as UAE President, Sheikh Zayed had continued to visit their small community, located on the shifting borderline between the desert and the city. He would sit on the sand with them, and ask if there was anything that they needed. On one occasion, he had asked for their help to load some pick-up trucks with food and other supplies, before driving around the nearby Liwa desert to hand-deliver these items to the people and families that still lived in the area.

"Death is a natural act," one of the elders was quoted as saying. "We all have to die one day, but there are some people, like [Sheikh Zayed], that you don't want to see die." A lot of people felt the same way, and by the end of November, over a thousand mourners per day were still lining up to visit Sheikh Zayed's grave in order to pay their own respects to the late UAE founder.

On December 2, 2004, the UAE marked its 33rd National Day. Falling just one month after Sheikh Zayed's passing, and while the country was still in mourning, the ordinarily jubilant occasion had taken on a somber and eerie tone that year. The official celebrations had been canceled, and the usually packed streets and parks were largely deserted. The traditional celebratory lights had not been strung up on the buildings of the UAE's cities. However, in an effort to reassure his fellow citizens that life would go on, the late Sheikh Zayed's eldest son and successor, Sheikh Khalifa, chose this melancholy occasion to issue his first address to the nation since succeeding his father as UAE President.

"Sheikh Zayed has passed away but his spirit and impressive legacy are immortal," said Sheikh Khalifa, thirty-three years to the day since the Rulers of the former Trucial States had come together in the face of the historic uncertainty that confronted them at the time. "His values and style of leadership will remain the beacon which will continue to guide us as we strengthen our federation and maintain the achievements and gains that the country has made in various spheres of development. As for us, we remain committed to serving this nation and to ensuring that even greater prosperity is achieved. Despite our bereavement, I would like to say that Zayed has not left us. For he has immortalized himself in our hearts through his noble deeds. He will remain among us forever."

References

CHAPTER 1

"a thing that has to happen": Records of the Emirates, Primary Documents 1820-1958, Volume 7, 1921-1935, edited by Penelope Tuson, Archive Editions [1990], p.149

exchange of diplomatic letters: Records of the Emirates, Primary Documents 1820-1958, Volume 7, 1921-1935, edited by Penelope Tuson, Archive Editions [1990], p.154

"With my father I would cross": Morris, Claud, The Desert Falcon: The story of H.H. Sheikh Zayed bin Sultan Al Nahiyan, President of the United Arab Emirates, The Outline Series of Books, 1976, p.23

CHAPTER 2

"He is to be found throughout the area": Heard-Bey, Frauke, From Trucial States to United Arab Emirates, Longman, 1982, p.25-26

"royal summer residence": https://abudhabiculture.ae/
en/experience/historic-landmarks/al-jahili-fort ["Al Jahili
Fort, one of the largest forts in the United Arab Emirates,
was built in the late 19th century by Sheikh Zayed bin
Khalifa the First (r. 1855-1909), both as a symbol of
power and as a royal summer residence."]

he may even have moved back there: Wilson, Graeme
H., Zayed: Man Who Built A Nation, National Archives,
2013, p.47

"saw at first hand the tribal issues": The Emirates
Center for Strategic Studies and Research, 'With United
Strength: H.H. Shaikh Zayid Bin Sultan Al Nahyan, The
Leader and the Nation,' principally authored by Andrew
Wheatcroft, 2004, p.64

"I loved riding and hunting": Morris, Claud, The Desert
Falcon: The story of H.H. Sheikh Zayed bin Sultan Al
Nahiyan, President of the United Arab Emirates, The
Outline Series of Books, 1976, p.21

"The boy would go up on Jebel Hafeet": Morris, Claud,
The Desert Falcon: The story of H.H. Sheikh Zayed
bin Sultan Al Nahiyan, President of the United Arab
Emirates, The Outline Series of Books, 1976, p.23-24

CHAPTER 3

"The foremost measure of a coastal ruler's strength":
Said Zahlan, Rosemarie, The Origins of the United Arab
Emirates: A Political and Social History of the Trucial
States, 1978, p.6

"Two days later we called on Shaikh Zayed": Henderson,
Edward, This Strange Eventful History: Memoirs of
Earlier Days in the UAE and Oman, Quartet Books,
1988, p.57, parentheses added

Al Saruj incident: The Emirates Center for Strategic
Studies and Research, 'With United Strength: H.H.
Shaikh Zayid Bin Sultan Al Nahyan, The Leader and
the Nation,' principally authored by Andrew Wheatcroft,
2004, p.80-83; Tammam, Hamdi, 'Zayed bin Sultan
Al-Nahyan: The Leader and the March,' Second Edition,
1983, p.59, p.61-62.

"I greeted them and exchanged the news with Zayid":
Thesiger, Wilfred, Arabian Sands, [New Ed.], Penguin,
London, 2007, p.268-269

"the Arabs are a race which produces its best . . .":
Thesiger, Wilfred, Arabian Sands, [New Ed.], Penguin,
London, 2007, p.97

"an Arabian nightmare, the final disillusionment":
Thesiger, Wilfred, Arabian Sands, [New Ed.], Penguin,
London, 2007, Preface to edition published in 1984

"reconciled to the inevitable changes": Thesiger, Wilfred,
Arabian Sands, [New Ed.], Penguin, London, 2007,
Preface to edition published in 1991, p.9

CHAPTER 4

Bedside reconciliation: Records of the Emirates, volume
unknown, Archive Editions [1990], p.16 ["Relations
between Abu Dhabi and Dubai continued strained until
1952 when the Rulers became reconciled at the bedside
of Zaid who was being treated for measles in the Dubai
hospital."]; Hawley, Donald, The Trucial States, George
Allen & Unwin Ltd, 1970, p.149

"pawned his wife's jewels": Records of the Emirates,
Primary Documents 1820-1958, Volume 9, 1947-1958,
edited by Penelope Tuson, Archive Editions [1990],
p.408-409, Memo from Political Agency Trucial States,
Dubai, to British Residency, Bahrain, 9 March 1954
(1011/2/54)

"Unfortunately even if it is true": Records of the
Emirates, Primary Documents 1820-1958, Volume 9,
1947-1958, edited by Penelope Tuson, Archive Editions

[1990], p.407, Memo from Political Agency Trucial
States, Dubai, to British Residency, Bahrain, 9 March
1954 (1011/2/54)

"Sheikh Shakhbut would hold forth on any subject":
Henderson, Edward, This Strange Eventful History:
Memoirs of Earlier Days in the UAE and Oman, Quartet
Books, 1988, p.19

first to invite foreign geologists: Morton, Michael
Quentin, Keepers of the Golden Shore: A History of
the United Arab Emirates, Reaktion Books Ltd, 2016,
p.134-135

international arbitration in Paris: Said Zahlan,
Rosemarie, The Origins of the United Arab Emirates: A
Political and Social History of the Trucial States, 1978,
p.177, 182, 193

heated dispute within his own family: Records of the
Emirates, Primary Documents 1820-1958, Volume 9,
1947-1958, edited by Penelope Tuson, Archive Editions
[1990], p.419-421, Memo from British Residency,
Bahrain, to The Right Honourable Anthony Eden, M.C.,
M.P., 15 April 1954 (10154/39/54)

"Sheikh Zaid said quite simply that he was glad . . . ":
Records of the Emirates, Primary Documents 1820-1958,

Volume 9, 1947-1958, edited by Penelope Tuson, Archive Editions [1990], p.420, Memo from British Residency, Bahrain, to The Right Honourable Anthony Eden, M.C., M.P., 15 April 1954 (10154/39/54)

"Whoever rules in Abu Dhabi it is": Records of the Emirates, Primary Documents 1820-1958, Volume 9, 1947-1958, edited by Penelope Tuson, Archive Editions [1990], p.414, M.S. Buckmaster to Burrows, 6 May 1954 (1016/4)

"Zaid's opinion is that for Shakhbut's . . ." Records of the Emirates, Primary Documents 1820-1958, Volume 9, 1947-1958, edited by Penelope Tuson, Archive Editions [1990], p.414, M.S. Buckmaster to Burrows, 6 May 1954 (1016/4)

Details of arbitration in Geneva: Morton, Michael, Buraimi: The Struggle for Power, Influence and Oil in Arabia, p.160, p.161-163, p.165, p.166, p.169, p.170-172

a force of around one hundred men: Henderson, Edward, This Strange Eventful History: Memoirs of Earlier Days in the UAE and Oman, Quartet Books, 1988, p.158-159; Morton, Michael, Buraimi: The Struggle for Power, Influence and Oil in Arabia, p.181

One shot was fired but no lives were lost: Morton, Michael, Buraimi: The Struggle for Power, Influence and Oil in Arabia, p.181

watched on through binoculars: Henderson, Edward, This Strange Eventful History: Memoirs of Earlier Days in the UAE and Oman, Quartet Books, 1988, p.163

contact was soon established: Henderson, Edward, This Strange Eventful History: Memoirs of Earlier Days in the UAE and Oman, Quartet Books, 1988, p.163-166

leaders of the resistance finally surrendered: The Emirates Center for Strategic Studies and Research, 'With United Strength: H.H. Shaikh Zayid Bin Sultan Al Nahyan, The Leader and the Nation,' principally authored by Andrew Wheatcroft, 2004, p.94; Henderson, Edward, This Strange Eventful History: Memoirs of Earlier Days in the UAE and Oman, Quartet Books, 1988, p.166

the lives of nine men: http://trucialomanscouts.org/ TOS/About.html ["... with 9 people killed in October 1956 [*sic*] including 7 Saudi policemen/military personnel and 2 TOS paramilitary troops"]

Documents and cash: British Hansard, HC Deb 07 November 1955 vol 545 cc1462-3

"As they approached Shaikh Zayed": Henderson, Edward, Arabian Destiny: The Complete Autobiography, Motivate Publishing, 1999, p.229-230; also quoted in abridged form in The Emirates Center for Strategic Studies and Research, 'With United Strength: H.H. Shaikh Zayid Bin Sultan Al Nahyan, The Leader and the Nation,' principally authored by Andrew Wheatcroft, 2004, p.95

CHAPTER 5

Shortly before 9:45 a.m.: Records of the Emirates, Primary Documents 1820-1958, Volume 9, 1947-1958, edited by Penelope Tuson, Archive Editions [1990], p.235, Minutes of the Eighth Meeting of the Trucial Council held in the Political Agency on 8th November 1955.

"As the Shaikhdoms develop": Records of the Emirates, Primary Documents 1820-1958, Volume 9, 1947-1958, edited by Penelope Tuson, Archive Editions [1990], p.77, British post-war policy, Memo from British Residency, Bahrain, to His Majesty's Principal Secretary of State for Foreign Affairs, 29 January 1951, No.13 (1082/2)

"tends to appreciate individual attention": Records of the Emirates, Primary Documents 1820-1958, Volume 9, 1947-1958, edited by Penelope Tuson, Archive Editions [1990], p.201, Memo from the Political Agency Trucial

States to the Political Resident, Bahrain, 5 July 1954, Despatch No.5 (10110/13/54)

At the fourth Trucial States Council meeting: Records of the Emirates, Primary Documents 1820-1958, Volume 9, 1947-1958, edited by Penelope Tuson, Archive Editions [1990], p.189, The Trucial States Council, Memo from Political Agency Trucial States, Sharjah, to Political Resident, Bahrain, 1 December 1953, Despatch No.4 (0228/20/53)

fifth meeting in July 1954: Records of the Emirates, Primary Documents 1820-1958, Volume 9, 1947-1958, edited by Penelope Tuson, Archive Editions [1990], p.201, Memo from the Political Agency Trucial States to the Political Resident, Bahrain, 5 July 1954, Despatch No.5 (10110/13/54)

"Even the Ruler of Abu Dhabi": Records of the Emirates, Primary Documents 1820-1958, Volume 9, 1947-1958, edited by Penelope Tuson, Archive Editions [1990], p.201, Memo from the Political Agency Trucial States to the Political Resident, Bahrain, 5 July 1954, Despatch No.5 (10110/13/54), parentheses added

"Abu Dhabi did not have such things": Records of the Emirates, Primary Documents 1820-1958, Volume 9, 1947-1958, edited by Penelope Tuson, Archive Editions

[1990], p.212, Minutes of the Fifth Meeting of the Trucial Council held in the Political Agency Residence on 25-6-1954

"caused genuine amusement to his fellows": Records of the Emirates, Primary Documents 1820-1958, Volume 9, 1947-1958, edited by Penelope Tuson, Archive Editions [1990], p.201, Memo from the Political Agency Trucial States to the Political Resident, Bahrain, 5 July 1954, Despatch No.5 (10110/13/54)

a portion of the potential funds: Records of the Emirates, Primary Documents 1820-1958, Volume 9, 1947-1958, edited by Penelope Tuson, Archive Editions [1990], p.192, Minutes of the Fourth Meeting of the Trucial Council at the Political Agency, Sharjah, on the 17th November, 1953

"The Chairman was concerned": Records of the Emirates, Primary Documents 1820-1958, Volume 9, 1947-1958, edited by Penelope Tuson, Archive Editions [1990], p.239, Minutes of the Eighth Meeting of the Trucial Council Held in the Political Agency on 8th November 1955

sixteen thousand Trucial State citizens: Records of the Emirates, Primary Documents 1820-1958, Volume 9, 1947-1958, edited by Penelope Tuson, Archive Editions

[1990], p.227, Minutes of the Seventh Meeting of the Trucial Council Held in the Political Agency on 23rd and 24th August 1955

"There were a lot of dreams I was dreaming . . .": Quoted in many sources, including "Sheikh Zayed bin Sultan Al Nahyan - A Special Tribute", publisher not identified but appears to be a National Media Council publication.

Sheikh Hazza and Sheikh Zayed: Al-Dhahiri, Shamsa Hamad, "Sheikh Hazza Bin Sultan Bin Zayed Al-Nahyan (1905-1958)", Liwa: Journal of the National Archives, Volume 6, Number 12, December 2014, p.29, p.45-46

evening of March 28, 1958: The National, Special Report, The Day The Oil Came, words by James Langton, published 28 March 2018; Abu Dhabi National Oil Company, Our History, https://www.adnoc.ae/en/about-us/our-history

barbed wire: Dycke, Gertrude, The Oasis: Al Ain memoirs of 'Doctora Latifa', Motivate Publishing, 1995, p.83

"In the village, the locals would sleep": Dycke, Gertrude, The Oasis: Al Ain memoirs of 'Doctora Latifa', Motivate Publishing, 1995, p.42

Abdul Hafeez Khan: Al Hameli, Asmaa, 'The man who realised Sheikh Zayed's dream of a desert turned green,' The National, 8 June 2015

breeding program for the Arabian oryx: Hellyer, Peter and Aspinall, Simon, 'Zayed: Caring Environmentalist,' Tribulus, Journal of the Emirates Natural History Group, Vol. 14.2, Autumn/Winter 2004, p.4

one of the largest herds: Hanif, Nadeem, 'Arabian Oryx thriving at Abu Dhabi sanctuary,' The National, 3 February 2015

Observations of J.P. Tripp: Unpublished FO 371/163025 33829, J.P. Tripp, Economic Secretary's Visit to Abu Dhabi, October 18-25, 1962, as edited and quoted in The Emirates Center for Strategic Studies and Research, 'With United Strength: H.H. Shaikh Zayid Bin Sultan Al Nahyan, The Leader and the Nation,' principally authored by Andrew Wheatcroft, 2004, p.105.

construction of the town's first road: Wilson, Graeme H., Zayed: Man Who Built A Nation, National Archives, 2013, p.62-63; The Emirates Center for Strategic Studies and Research, 'With United Strength: H.H. Shaikh Zayid Bin Sultan Al Nahyan, The Leader and the Nation,' principally authored by Andrew Wheatcroft, 2004, p.109-110

"In 1960 the inhabitants still lived from hand to mouth": Al-Fahim, Mohammed, From Rags to Riches: A Story of Abu Dhabi, The London Centre of Arab Studies, 1995, p.47, parentheses added

CHAPTER 6
"I see nothing around me or in the health of Shakhbut": Records of the Emirates, 1966-1971, Volume 1, 1966, edited by A.L. P. Burdett, Archive Editions [2002], p.37, Lamb to Phillips, 19 January 1966 (1941/66)

lashed out at British officials: Records of the Emirates, 1966-1971, Volume 1, 1966, edited by A.L. P. Burdett, Archive Editions [2002], p.88, Lamb to Luce, 4 June 1966 (1011/66G)

profile in an American magazine: Green, Timothy, "The Shekels of Sheik Shakhbut", LIFE, 3 May 1963, p.49-61

secret memo: Records of the Emirates, 1966-1971, Volume 1, 1966, edited by A.L. P. Burdett, Archive Editions [2002], p.96, Green to Prime Minister, 22 December 1964, PM/64/152

" . . . so long as Sheikh Shakhbut is the Ruler,": Records of the Emirates, 1966-1971, Volume 1, 1966, edited by

A.L. P. Burdett, Archive Editions [2002], p.96, Green to Prime Minister, 22 December 1964, PM/64/152

Visit from Sheikh Khalid: Records of the Emirates, 1966-1971, Volume 1, 1966, edited by A.L. P. Burdett, Archive Editions [2002], p.38, Lamb to Luce, 13 February 1966

a man of considerable charm and intelligence: Records of the Emirates, 1966-1971, Volume 1, 1966, edited by A.L. P. Burdett, Archive Editions [2002], p.42, Annex II of Lamb to Weir, 23 April 1966 (1941/66)

a jetty and crucial electricity projects: Records of the Emirates, 1966-1971, Volume 1, 1966, edited by A.L. P. Burdett, Archive Editions [2002], p.92, British Political Agency to Luce, 4 June 1966 (1041/66)

pledged extravagant gifts: Records of the Emirates, 1966-1971, Volume 1, 1966, edited by A.L. P. Burdett, Archive Editions [2002], p.63, Lamb to Luce, 30 April 1966 (1033/66)

an even more generous financial gift: Records of the Emirates, 1966-1971, Volume 1, 1966, edited by A.L. P. Burdett, Archive Editions [2002], p.93, Parkes to Luce, 21 June 1966 (1033/66)

Rising oil revenues: Records of the Emirates, 1966-1971, Volume 1, 1966, edited by A.L. P. Burdett, Archive Editions [2002], p.66, Annex to Lamb to Luce, 30 April 1966 (1033/66)

only £2m was spent: Records of the Emirates, 1966-1971, Volume 1, 1966, edited by A.L. P. Burdett, Archive Editions [2002], p.66, Annex to Lamb to Luce, 30 April 1966 (1033/66)

plan to pressure Sheikh Shakhbut: Records of the Emirates, 1966-1971, Volume 1, 1966, edited by A.L. P. Burdett, Archive Editions [2002], p.45-46, Lamb to Luce, 21 May 1966 (1013/66)

seventy-three family members: Records of the Emirates, 1966-1971, Volume 1, 1966, edited by A.L. P. Burdett, Archive Editions [2002], p.86, Lamb to Luce, 4 June 1966 (1941/66)

had the two office safes moved: Records of the Emirates, 1966-1971, Volume 1, 1966, edited by A.L. P. Burdett, Archive Editions [2002], p.88, Lamb to Luce, 4 June 1966 (1011/66G)

Sheikh Zayed departed Abu Dhabi and travelled to the UK: Records of the Emirates, 1966-1971, Volume 1, 1966, edited by A.L. P. Burdett, Archive Editions [2002],

p.41, Lamb to Weir, 23 April 1966 (1941/66); Records of
the Emirates, 1966-1971, Volume 1, 1966, edited by A.L.
P. Burdett, Archive Editions [2002], p.82, Confidential
Briefing Note from Weir, 29 June 1966

Sheikh Zayed refused this request: Records of the
Emirates, 1966-1971, Volume 1, 1966, edited by A.L. P.
Burdett, Archive Editions [2002], p.76, Lamb to Luce, 29
May 1966 (1941/66)

Hall Barn: Abbey, Sue, "The Hall Barn Estate",
Beaconsfield & District Historical Society

Summary of itinerary in UK: Records of the Emirates,
1966-1971, Volume 1, 1966, edited by A.L. P. Burdett,
Archive Editions [2002], p.82, Weir to unknown, 29 June
1966

meeting at the Foreign and Commonwealth Office:
Records of the Emirates, 1966-1971, Volume 1, 1966,
edited by A.L. P. Burdett, Archive Editions [2002], p.44,
Lamb to Weir, 21 May 1966 (1941/66)

"a trained and efficient body of men . . .": Records of
the Emirates, 1966-1971, Volume 1, 1966, edited by
A.L. P. Burdett, Archive Editions [2002], p.94, Nuttall to
Balfour-Paul, 16 July 1966 (1941/66)

"Frankly I didn't wish, or desire": Morris, Claud, The Desert Falcon: The story of H.H. Sheikh Zayed bin Sultan Al Nahiyan, President of the United Arab Emirates, The Outline Series of Books, 1976, p.68 and p.70, parentheses added

"Impelled by lamentable condition": Records of the Emirates, 1966-1971, Volume 1, 1966, edited by A.L. P. Burdett, Archive Editions [2002], p.101, Nuttall to Foreign Office, 5 August 1966 (No.103)

on August 6, 1966, the Acting Political Resident: Records of the Emirates, 1966-1971, Volume 1, 1966, edited by A.L. P. Burdett, Archive Editions [2002], p.102, Guidance from Foreign and Commonwealth Office to Certain Missions, 6 August 1966 (Guidance No. 241); Morris, Claud, The Desert Falcon: The story of H.H. Sheikh Zayed bin Sultan Al Nahiyan, President of the United Arab Emirates, The Outline Series of Books, 1976, p.69

Blind in one eye: Records of the Emirates, 1966-1971, Volume 1, 1966, edited by A.L. P. Burdett, Archive Editions [2002], p.35, Lamb to Phillips, 5 January 1966 (1941/66)

Sheikh Zayed ended up speaking to his brother: Records of the Emirates, 1966-1971, Volume 1, 1966, edited by

A.L. P. Burdett, Archive Editions [2002], p.139, Lamb to Balfour-Paul, 20 August 1966 (1011/66); Morris, Claud, The Desert Falcon: The story of H.H. Sheikh Zayed bin Sultan Al Nahiyan, President of the United Arab Emirates, The Outline Series of Books, 1976, p.70

Sheikh Shakhbut's departure: Records of the Emirates, 1966-1971, Volume 1, 1966, edited by A.L. P. Burdett, Archive Editions [2002], p.116, Foreign Office to Kuwait, 11 August 1966 (1016/31); Morris, Claud, The Desert Falcon: The story of H.H. Sheikh Zayed bin Sultan Al Nahiyan, President of the United Arab Emirates, The Outline Series of Books, 1976, p.70

His immediate family followed: Records of the Emirates, 1966-1971, Volume 1, 1966, edited by A.L. P. Burdett, Archive Editions [2002], p.115, Foreign Office to Kuwait, 11 August 1966 (1016/31)

two squadrons of Trucial Oman Scouts: Records of the Emirates, 1966-1971, Volume 1, 1966, edited by A.L. P. Burdett, Archive Editions [2002], p.116, Foreign Office to Kuwait, 11 August 1966 (1016/31)

CHAPTER 7
He barely left the confines: Records of the Emirates, Volume 1: 1966, edited by A.L. P. Burdett, Archive

Editions [2002], p.123, Balfour-Paul to British Political Agency, Abu Dhabi, 13 August 1966 (1011/66)

announced transformative plans: Records of the Emirates, Volume 1: 1966, edited by A.L. P. Burdett, Archive Editions [2002], p.114, Nuttall to Foreign Office, 11 August 1966

direct cash payments: Wilson, Graeme H., Zayed: Man Who Built A Nation, National Archives, 2013, p.67-68

the establishment of dedicated departments: Hawley, Donald, The Trucial States, George Allen & Unwin Ltd, 1970, p.248-249

"I felt that only by establishing a probationary period": Morris, Claud, The Desert Falcon: The story of H.H. Sheikh Zayed bin Sultan Al Nahiyan, President of the United Arab Emirates, The Outline Series of Books, 1976, p.76

the regional reaction: Records of the Emirates, Volume 1: 1966, edited by A.L. P. Burdett, Archive Editions [2002], p.107, Bahrain telegram No.531 to Foreign Office, 8 August 1966; Records of the Emirates, Volume 1: 1966, edited by A.L. P. Burdett, Archive Editions [2002], p.110, Kuwait telegraph No.354 to Foreign Office, 9 August 1966: Records of the Emirates, Volume 1: 1966, edited by A.L. P. Burdett, Archive Editions [2002], p.129, Jedda to Foreign Office, 15 August 1966

lodged a formal protest: Records of the Emirates, Volume 1: 1966, edited by A.L. P. Burdett, Archive Editions [2002], p.138, Balfour-Paul to Political Agency, Abu Dhabi (1011/66), 20 August 1966

Sheikh Rashid had successfully turned Dubai into a vibrant trading hub: Hawley, Donald, The Trucial States, George Allen & Unwin Ltd, 1970, p.246-248; Records of the Emirates, Volume 5: 1970, edited by A.L. P. Burdett, Archive Editions [2002], p.87-88, General Background on Dubai; Morton, Michael Quentin, Keepers of the Golden Shore: A History of the United Arab Emirates, Reaktion Books Ltd, 2016, p.175; Wilson, Graham, Father of Dubai: Sheikh Rashid bin Saeed Al-Maktoum, Media Prima, 1999, p.87, p.89, p.131

"He lives simply and works hard": Records of the Emirates, Volume 5: 1970, edited by A.L. P. Burdett, Archive Editions [2002], p.86-88, General Background on Dubai

"Sheikh Rashid does not speak English but": Records of the Emirates, Volume 5: 1970, edited by A.L. P. Burdett, Archive Editions [2002], p.83, Personality Notes, Shaikh Rashid bin Sa'id al Maktum, Ruler of Dubai

In his view, their participation in the deposal: Records
of the Emirates, Volume 1: 1966, edited by A.L. P.
Burdett, Archive Editions [2002], p.136, Bahrain
telegram No.566 to Foreign Office, 20 August 1966

leaders in the UAE would be echoing this sentiment:
Obama, Barack, A Promised Land, Crown, 2020, p.651

**Meeting with Sheikh Rashid and Sheikh Khalifa bin
Salman:** Records of the Emirates, Volume 1: 1966, edited
by A.L. P. Burdett, Archive Editions [2002], p.138-139,
Balfour-Paul to Political Agency, Abu Dhabi (1011/66),
20 August 1966

desire for friendship: Records of the Emirates, Volume 1:
1966, edited by A.L. P. Burdett, Archive Editions [2002],
p.146, Abu Dhabi [Lamb] to Foreign Office [Arabian
Dept.], 25 August 1966

initial contribution of £500,000: Records of the
Emirates, Volume 2: 1967, edited by A.L. P. Burdett,
Archive Editions [2002], p.293, Lamb to Balfour-Paul
(1102/66), 22 August 1967

Sheikh Zayed would quadruple this contribution:
Records of the Emirates, Volume 2: 1967, edited by
A.L. P. Burdett, Archive Editions [2002], p.47, Lamb to
Crawford, 24 October 1967, enclosed with Crawford to

Brown, 15 November 1967; Heard-Bey, Frauke, From
Trucial States to United Arab Emirates, Longman, 1982,
p.323; Hawley, Donald, The Trucial States, George Allen
& Unwin Ltd, 1970, p.229

direct financial assistance to the Rulers: Records of
the Emirates, Volume 1: 1966, edited by A.L. P. Burdett,
Archive Editions [2002], p.135, Clark to Melhuish, 17
August 1966

sale of their own official postage stamps: Hawley,
Donald, The Trucial States, George Allen & Unwin Ltd,
1970, p.183, p.204

collection and return of the rifles: Records of the
Emirates, Volume 2: 1967, edited by A.L. P. Burdett,
Archive Editions [2002], p.403, Telegram No.079 from
Dubai to Abu Dhabi, 19 June 1967

correspondence from the period suggests: Records of
the Emirates, Volume 2: 1967, edited by A.L. P. Burdett,
Archive Editions [2002], p.408, Telegram No.26 from
Dubai to Foreign Office, 29 May 1967

"a man": Records of the Emirates, Volume 2: 1967, edited
by A.L. P. Burdett, Archive Editions [2002], p.29, Lamb
to Roberts (1011/67), 1 March 1967

"a good man": Records of the Emirates, Volume 2: 1967, edited by A.L. P. Burdett, Archive Editions [2002], p.393, Roberts to Lamb, 16 March 1967

"The difference between them I think": Records of the Emirates, Volume 2: 1967, edited by A.L. P. Burdett, Archive Editions [2002], p.393, Roberts to Lamb, 16 March 1967

"while Sheikh Zaid of Abu Dhabi rules essentially": Records of the Emirates, Volume 5: 1970, edited by A.L. P. Burdett, Archive Editions [2002], p.86, General Background on Dubai

considered Sheikh Rashid to be his elder: Records of the Emirates, Volume 3: 1968, edited by A.L. P. Burdett, Archive Editions [2002], p.155, Lamb to Crawford, 20 March 1968

Similarities between Sheikh Zayed and Sheikh Rashid: Records of the Emirates, Volume 5: 1970, edited by A.L. P. Burdett, Archive Editions [2002], p.82-83, 'Personality Notes: Shaikh Rashid bin Sa'id al Maktum, Ruler of Dubai'; Records of the Emirates, Volume 5: 1970, edited by A.L. P. Burdett, Archive Editions [2002], p.85-92, General Background on Dubai; Wilson, Graham, Father of Dubai: Sheikh Rashid bin Saeed Al-Maktoum, Media

Prima, 1999, p.44, p.45, p.55, p.63-69, p.90-92, p.113, p.151

allowing his own palace to be used as an elementary school: Hawley, Donald, The Trucial States, George Allen & Unwin Ltd, 1970, p.234-235

In May 1967, Sheikh Zayed reached out: Records of the Emirates, Volume 2: 1967, edited by A.L. P. Burdett, Archive Editions [2002], p.415, Dubai/Abu Dhabi Relations, 2 July 1967

a direct backchannel: Records of the Emirates, Volume 2: 1967, edited by A.L. P. Burdett, Archive Editions [2002], p.29, Lamb to Roberts (1011/67), 1 March 1967

By the end of 1967, Sheikh Rashid was secretly: Records of the Emirates, Volume 2: 1967, edited by A.L. P. Burdett, Archive Editions [2002], p.50, Roberts to Lamb (1014/67C), 21 December 1967

First anniversary celebrations: Records of the Emirates, Volume 2: 1967, edited by A.L. P. Burdett, Archive Editions [2002], p.38-43, Nuttall to Crawford, 12 August 1967

CHAPTER 8

a strong British presence would be retained: Records of the Emirates, Volume 5: 1970, edited by A.L. P. Burdett, Archive Editions [2002], p.28, Valedictory Despatch from Sir Stewart Crawford, Political Resident in the Persian Gulf, 3 August 1970

Reaction to British withdrawal plans: Records of the Emirates, Volume 3: 1968, edited by A.L. P. Burdett, Archive Editions [2002], p.223, Bahrain to Foreign Office, 11 January 1968

Trucial States population figures: Records of the Emirates, Volume 5: 1970, edited by A.L. P. Burdett, Archive Editions [2002], p.325, Approximate population of the Trucial States in 1968; Data from 1968 census also cited in Hawley, Donald, The Trucial States, George Allen & Unwin Ltd, 1970, Appendix A.2., p.277

Meeting with Sheikh Rashid on January 22: Records of the Emirates, Volume 3: 1968, edited by A.L. P. Burdett, Archive Editions [2002], p.36, Lamb to Crawford, 24 January 1968

enthusiastic but somewhat vague communique: Records of the Emirates, Volume 3: 1968, edited by A.L. P. Burdett, Archive Editions [2002], p.29-31, Translation of Text of Joint Communique, 22 January 1968

Offer to cover cost of military presence: Records of the
Emirates, Volume 3: 1968, edited by A.L. P. Burdett,
Archive Editions [2002], p.234, Bahrain to Foreign
Office, 24 January 1968; Records of the Emirates, Volume
3: 1968, edited by A.L. P. Burdett, Archive Editions
[2002], p.238, Lamb to Crawford, 24 January 1968;
Records of the Emirates, Volume 3: 1968, edited by A.L.
P. Burdett, Archive Editions [2002], p.240, Record of
Conversation between the Political Resident and the
Ruler of Abu Dhabi on 30 January 1968

settled a longstanding offshore boundary dispute:
United Nations, "Offshore boundary agreement between
Abu Dhabi and Dubai, 18 February 1968"; Records of
the Emirates, Volume 5: 1970, edited by A.L. P. Burdett,
Archive Editions [2002], p.90, General Background on
Dubai

subsidizing the provision of electricity: Records of the
Emirates, Volume 3: 1968, edited by A.L. P. Burdett,
Archive Editions [2002], p.53, Roberts to Balfour-Paul,
22 February 1968

Union Accord: Records of the Emirates, Volume 3: 1968,
edited by A.L. P. Burdett, Archive Editions [2002], p.50,
"Text of Communique issued by Rulers of Dubai and
Abu Dhabi on 18 February," quoted in Dubai to Foreign
Office, 19 February 1968

Speaking to British officials shortly after the deal:
Records of the Emirates, Volume 3: 1968, edited by A.L.
P. Burdett, Archive Editions [2002], p.148-149, Lamb to
Crawford, 7 March 1968

expressed varying degrees of interest in joining:
Records of the Emirates, Volume 3: 1968, edited by A.L.
P. Burdett, Archive Editions [2002], p.149, Lamb to
Crawford, 7 March 1968

putting pen to paper: Exhibition display at Etihad
Museum ["This meeting was soon followed by another
historical meeting, on the 28th of March 1968, in Al
Madam in Sharjah between Sheikh Zayed bin Sultan Al
Nahyan and Sheikh Khalid bin Mohammed Al Qasimi,
the Ruler of Sharjah. The two Rulers signed an agreement
similar to the Abu Dhabi-Dubai Agreement, one that
also emphasized a federal approach."]

Interview with British newspaper in October 1968:
Heard-Bey, Frauke, From Trucial States to United Arab
Emirates, Longman, 1982, p.349

**"No one can persuade us that there is some magic
number":** Morris, Claud, The Desert Falcon: The story of
H.H. Sheikh Zayed bin Sultan Al Nahiyan, President of
the United Arab Emirates, The Outline Series of Books,
1976, p.79-80

driving multiple horses: Records of the Emirates, Volume 3: 1968, edited by A.L. P. Burdett, Archive Editions [2002], p.148, Lamb to Crawford, 7 March 1968

gamely attempted to project a film: Records of the Emirates, Volume 3: 1968, edited by A.L. P. Burdett, Archive Editions [2002], p.118, Treadwell to Weir, 7 July 1968

personal interest in the planning of Abu Dhabi City: Bani Hashim, Alamira Reem, Planning Abu Dhabi: An Urban History, Routledge, 2019, p.90

creation of decentralized villages: Tammam, Hamdi, 'Zayed bin Sultan Al-Nahyan: The Leader and the March,' Second Edition, 1983, p.94

monthly financial stipends and offering transport: Maitra, Jayanti, Zayed: From Challenges to Union, Center for Documentation & Research, 2007, p.127

"remark designed for public consumption": Records of the Emirates, 1966-1971, Volume 1, 1966, edited by A.L. P. Burdett, Archive Editions [2002], p.109, Nuttall to Bahrain and FCO, 9 August 1966 (No. 106)

a looser union that involved as many members as possible: Records of the Emirates, Volume 5: 1970, edited by A.L. P. Burdett, Archive Editions [2002], p.93, Record of Conversation between the Foreign and Commonwealth Secretary and the Ruler of Dubai at the Foreign and Commonwealth Office, 31 July 1970

"neither intelligent nor tough enough": Records of the Emirates, Volume 5: 1970, edited by A.L. P. Burdett, Archive Editions [2002], p.17, Persian Gulf: Annual Review for 1970, Diplomatic Report No. 19/71, 1 January 1971

"difficult to see Zaid as the leader": Records of the Emirates, Volume 5: 1970, edited by A.L. P. Burdett, Archive Editions [2002], p.18, Persian Gulf: Annual Review for 1970, Diplomatic Report No. 19/71, 1 January 1971

almost ten-thousand-strong Abu Dhabi Defence Force: The Emirates Center for Strategic Studies and Research, 'With United Strength: H.H. Shaikh Zayid Bin Sultan Al Nahyan, The Leader and the Nation,' principally authored by Andrew Wheatcroft, 2004, p.221

It is unclear whether the Trucial State Rulers would have produced: A similar observation was also made in Heard-Bey, Frauke, From Trucial States to United Arab Emirates, Longman, 1982, p.371

whirlwind tour of the Emirates: Wilson, Graeme H., Zayed: Man Who Built A Nation, National Archives, 2013, p.84

a series of transformative water and electricity projects: Wilson, Graeme H., Zayed: Man Who Built A Nation, National Archives, 2013, p.84, p.90 and p.107

"Any Emirate with three schools today is going to have forty": Morris, Claud, The Desert Falcon: The story of H.H. Sheikh Zayed bin Sultan Al Nahiyan, President of the United Arab Emirates, The Outline Series of Books, 1976, p.77-78

"*sine qua non* [ie. an essential condition]": Records of the Emirates, Volume 5: 1970, edited by A.L. P. Burdett, Archive Editions [2002], p.276, Consultations with the Shah, 10 July 1970

Iran fully intended to seize them: Records of the Emirates, Volume 5: 1970, edited by A.L. P. Burdett, Archive Editions [2002], p.335, Policy in the Persian Gulf, 16 November 1970

Attack on Deputy Ruler of Sharjah: The New York Times, "An Arab State Is Born Amid Persian Gulf Unrest," 3 December 1971

"Division is not natural to our people": Leadership:
Collection of Speeches, Stances, Meetings and
Instructions of H.H. Sheikh Zayed Bin Sultan
Al-Nahyan, President of the United Arab Emirates,
1971-1987, produced and published by Book and
Publishing Establishment, documented by Muhammed
Khaleel Al-Siksek, edited by Shams Al-Din Al-Doaifi,
p.41-42

CHAPTER 9

series of historic laws and decrees: Sheikh Zayed: Hopes
and Deeds, Book and Publishing Establishment, 1990,
p.20

Sharjah coup attempt: Taryam, Abdullah Omran, The
Establishment of the United Arab Emirates 1950-85,
Routledge (2017), originally published by Croon Helm
(1987), p.191; Al Maktoum, Mohammed bin Rashid,
My Story: 50 Memories from Fifty Years of Service, The
Executive Office/Explorer Publishing and Distribution,
2019, p.122

"resolve the matter quickly": Al Maktoum, Mohammed
bin Rashid, My Story: 50 Memories from Fifty Years of
Service, The Executive Office/Explorer Publishing and
Distribution, 2019, p.121-123

rolling out basic infrastructure and services: The
Emirates Center for Strategic Studies and Research,
'With United Strength: H.H. Shaikh Zayid Bin Sultan
Al Nahyan, The Leader and the Nation,' principally
authored by Andrew Wheatcroft, 2004, p.202; Sheikh
Zayed: Hopes and Deeds, Book and Publishing
Establishment, 1990, "Speech of His Highness Sheikh
Zayed Bin Sultan Al Nahyan, President of the U.A.E.,
at the opening of the second ordinary session of the first
legislative section" (20 November 1972), p.24-36

electricity to every house: Sheikh Zayed: Hopes and
Deeds, Book and Publishing Establishment, 1990, p.46

**In its first three years, the UAE Government would
pass:** Taryam, Abdullah Omran, The Establishment of
the United Arab Emirates 1950-85, Routledge (2017),
originally published by Croon Helm (1987), p.217-218;
Sheikh Zayed: Hopes and Deeds, Book and Publishing
Establishment, 1990, "Speech of His Highness Sheikh
Zayed Bin Sultan Al Nahyan, President of the U.A.E.,
at the opening of the second ordinary session of the first
legislative section" (20 November 1972), p.236

"Our foreign policy sets four objectives": UAE Ministry
of Information and Culture, Majmu'at Tasriha Ahadith
wa Tashrihat Sahib al Sumu al Shaikh Zayed bin Sultan
al-Nahyan, p.30-31, quoted in Emirates Center for

Strategic Studies and Research, 'With United Strength: H.H. Shaikh Zayid Bin Sultan Al Nahyan, The Leader and the Nation,' 2004, p.219, translation edited for clarity

"We must not rely on oil alone": Leadership: Collection of Speeches, Stances, Meetings and Instructions of H.H. Sheikh Zayed Bin Sultan Al-Nahyan, President of the United Arab Emirates, 1971-1987, produced and published by Book and Publishing Establishment, documented by Muhammed Khaleel Al-Siksek, edited by Shams Al-Din Al-Doaifi, p.159

Series of landmark projects in Dubai from 1971-1985: The pivotal role of Sheikh Rashid in the conception and development of several of these projects is discussed in detail in Wilson, Graham, Father of Dubai: Sheikh Rashid bin Saeed Al-Maktoum, Media Prima, 1999

"Whatever buildings, installations, schools or hospitals we erect": Leadership: Collection of Speeches, Stances, Meetings and Instructions of H.H. Sheikh Zayed Bin Sultan Al-Nahyan, President of the United Arab Emirates, 1971-1987, produced and published by Book and Publishing Establishment, documented by Muhammed Khaleel Al-Siksek, edited by Shams Al-Din Al-Doaifi, p.48, translation edited for clarity

isolated armed clashes: Taryam, Abdullah Omran, The Establishment of the United Arab Emirates 1950-85, Routledge (2017), originally published by Croon Helm (1987), p.228

"There is no conflict between the federal and local ministries": Leadership: Collection of Speeches, Stances, Meetings and Instructions of H.H. Sheikh Zayed Bin Sultan Al-Nahyan, President of the United Arab Emirates, 1971-1987, produced and published by Book and Publishing Establishment, documented by Muhammed Khaleel Al-Siksek, edited by Shams Al-Din Al-Doaifi, p.67

Key elements of and reaction to "Problems and Obstacles in the Way of Union" document: Taryam, Abdullah Omran, The Establishment of the United Arab Emirates 1950-85, Routledge (2017), originally published by Croon Helm (1987), p.221-223

the UAE flag was now flying exclusively across the country: Sheikh Zayed: Hopes and Deeds, Book and Publishing Establishment, 1990, "Speech of His Highness Sheikh Zayed Bin Sultan Al Nahyan, President of the U.A.E., at the opening of the third ordinary session of the second legislative section" (18 November 1975), p.66

hesitant to relinquish greater control: Taryam, Abdullah Omran, The Establishment of the United Arab Emirates 1950-85, Routledge (2017), originally published by Croon Helm (1987), p.224

"The work of federating brings many new horizons": Leadership: Collection of Speeches, Stances, Meetings and Instructions of H.H. Sheikh Zayed Bin Sultan Al-Nahyan, President of the United Arab Emirates, 1971-1987, produced and published by Book and Publishing Establishment, documented by Muhammed Khaleel Al-Siksek, edited by Shams Al-Din Al-Doaifi, p.65-66

Renewal of provisional constitution and outstanding issues: Taryam, Abdullah Omran, The Establishment of the United Arab Emirates 1950-85, Routledge (2017), originally published by Croon Helm (1987), p.236

"the first to back whatever president is chosen": Leadership: Collection of Speeches, Stances, Meetings and Instructions of H.H. Sheikh Zayed Bin Sultan Al-Nahyan, President of the United Arab Emirates, 1971-1987, produced and published by Book and Publishing Establishment, documented by Muhammed Khaleel Al-Siksek, edited by Shams Al-Din Al-Doaifi, p.57

Reaction to Sheikh Zayed's decision: Chronicle of
Progress, Trident Press (1996), edited by Al Abed,
Ibrahim, Vine, Paula and Al Jabali, Abdullah, p.99-103;
Wilson, Graeme H., Zayed: Man Who Built A Nation,
National Archives, 2013, p.263, p.268; Tammam, Hamdi,
'Zayed bin Sultan Al-Nahyan: The Leader and the
March,' Second Edition, 1983, p.322-329.

personal visit from Sheikh Rashid: Chronicle of
Progress, Trident Press (1996), edited by Al Abed,
Ibrahim, Vine, Paula and Al Jabali, Abdullah, p.102

"I will give you an example": Leadership: Collection
of Speeches, Stances, Meetings and Instructions of
H.H. Sheikh Zayed Bin Sultan Al-Nahyan, President
of the United Arab Emirates, 1971-1987, produced
and published by Book and Publishing Establishment,
documented by Muhammed Khaleel Al-Siksek, edited by
Shams Al-Din Al-Doaifi, p.34

"If my brother Shakhbut was Ruler": Morris, Claud,
The Desert Falcon: The story of H.H. Sheikh Zayed
bin Sultan Al Nahiyan, President of the United Arab
Emirates, The Outline Series of Books, 1976, p.62

amendments to the provisional constitution: Chronicle
of Progress, Trident Press (1996), edited by Al Abed,
Ibrahim, Vine, Paula and Al Jabali, Abdullah, p.104

"God be praised . . . I do not wish to relinquish":
Leadership: Collection of Speeches, Stances, Meetings
and Instructions of H.H. Sheikh Zayed Bin Sultan
Al-Nahyan, President of the United Arab Emirates,
1971-1987, produced and published by Book and
Publishing Establishment, documented by Muhammed
Khaleel Al-Siksek, edited by Shams Al-Din Al-Doaifi,
p.33

**1979 Memorandum from FNC and Council of
Ministers:** Taryam, Abdullah Omran, The Establishment
of the United Arab Emirates 1950-85, Routledge (2017),
originally published by Croon Helm (1987), p.240-242

"Thousands of citizens from various walks of life":
Taryam, Abdullah Omran, The Establishment of the
United Arab Emirates 1950-85, Routledge (2017),
originally published by Croon Helm (1987), p.242-243

Sheikh Zayed's response to pro-unity demonstration:
Taryam, Abdullah Omran, The Establishment of the
United Arab Emirates 1950-85, Routledge (2017),
originally published by Croon Helm (1987), p.243

"The unification measures called for by our people":
Leadership: Collection of Speeches, Stances, Meetings
and Instructions of H.H. Sheikh Zayed Bin Sultan
Al-Nahyan, President of the United Arab Emirates,

1971-1987, produced and published by Book and
Publishing Establishment, documented by Muhammed
Khaleel Al-Siksek, edited by Shams Al-Din Al-Doaifi,
p.42, text in parentheses added for clarity

**Summary of and reaction to statements traded by
Governments of Abu Dhabi and Dubai:** Taryam,
Abdullah Omran, The Establishment of the United Arab
Emirates 1950-85, Routledge (2017), originally published
by Croon Helm (1987), p.244

Senior representatives of Kuwait and Saudi Arabia:
Taryam, Abdullah Omran, The Establishment of the
United Arab Emirates 1950-85, Routledge (2017),
originally published by Croon Helm (1987), p.244

a workable compromise had been reached: Taryam,
Abdullah Omran, The Establishment of the United Arab
Emirates 1950-85, Routledge (2017), originally published
by Croon Helm (1987), p.244

**agreed to commit fifty percent of their respective oil
income:** Chronicle of Progress, Trident Press (1996),
edited by Al Abed, Ibrahim, Vine, Paula and Al Jabali,
Abdullah, p.157

"Is there any federated state in our era": Leadership:
Collection of Speeches, Stances, Meetings and

Instructions of H.H. Sheikh Zayed Bin Sultan
Al-Nahyan, President of the United Arab Emirates,
1971-1987, produced and published by Book and
Publishing Establishment, documented by Muhammed
Khaleel Al-Siksek, edited by Shams Al-Din Al-Doaifi,
p.65-66

CHAPTER 10
"the ideal example for global Arab cooperation":
Sheikh Zayed: Hopes and Deeds, Book and Publishing
Establishment, 1990, p.107

"strict neutrality": Ottaway, David B., 'Arab Gulf States
Take Neutral Stance on Iran-Iraq War,' The Washington
Post, 1 June 1982.

"This war does not profit anyone": Leadership:
Collection of Speeches, Stances, Meetings and
Instructions of H.H. Sheikh Zayed Bin Sultan
Al-Nahyan President of the United Arab Emirates,
since 1971 to 1987, edited by Al-Doaifi Al-Din, Shams,
Book and Publishing Establishment, p.278, translation
amended for clarity

mediator in a series of disputes: Wilson, Graeme H.,
Zayed: Man Who Built A Nation, National Archives,
2013, p.307-313

"The security of the Gulf is the responsibility":
Leadership: Collection of Speeches, Stances, Meetings and Instructions of H.H. Sheikh Zayed Bin Sultan Al-Nahyan President of the United Arab Emirates, since 1971 to 1987, edited by Al-Doaifi Al-Din, Shams, Book and Publishing Establishment, p.137, translation amended for clarity

"The conference was decisive and binding":
Leadership: Collection of Speeches, Stances, Meetings and Instructions of H.H. Sheikh Zayed Bin Sultan Al-Nahyan President of the United Arab Emirates, since 1971 to 1987, edited by Al-Doaifi Al-Din, Shams, Book and Publishing Establishment, p.129, p.131

"the Emirates would never consider the question":
'Ford, Visiting Gulf, Is Told of Link Between Palestinians and Bases,' New York Times, 16 March 1981

"I have friendships and interests with the West":
Leadership: Collection of Speeches, Stances, Meetings and Instructions of H.H. Sheikh Zayed Bin Sultan Al-Nahyan President of the United Arab Emirates, since 1971 to 1987, edited by Al-Doaifi Al-Din, Shams, Book and Publishing Establishment, p.145

The UAE's federal budget was forty percent smaller:
Taryam, Abdullah Omran, The Establishment of the

United Arab Emirates 1950-85, Routledge (2017),
originally published by Croon Helm (1987), p.249

"The road so far, and on towards the future": Sheikh
Zayed: Hopes and Deeds, Book and Publishing
Establishment, 1990, p.134

"We are absolutely certain that the dissension":
Sheikh Zayed: Hopes and Deeds, Book and Publishing
Establishment, 1990, p.136

"Since Egypt is a part of the great Arab world":
Sheikh Zayed: Hopes and Deeds, Book and Publishing
Establishment, 1990, p.137

"a summer cloud, a passing thing": Chronicle of
Progress, edited by Al Abed, Ibrahim, Vine, Paula and Al
Jabali, Abdullah, Trident Press, 1996, p.322

Reports from inside the room: Kifner, John,
'Confrontation in the Gulf, Arab Vote to Send Troops to
Help Saudis; Boycott of Iraqi Oil is Reported Near 100%;
Baghdad Isolated,' New York Times, 11 August 1990

"Is it our duty to save the face": Wilson, Graeme H.,
Zayed: Man Who Built A Nation, National Archives,
2013, p.508

"political watershed in Gulf attitudes": Gordon, Michael R., 'Confrontation in the Gulf; Cheney, on Quick Tour, Reaches Agreement on More Bases in Gulf,' New York Times, 21 August 1990; 'United Arab Emirates Cooperates with U.S.', The Associated Press/Sun Sentinel, 21 August 1990

solidarity with Saudi Arabia: Gordon, Michael R., 'Confrontation in the Gulf; Cheney, on Quick Tour, Reaches Agreement on More Bases in Gulf,' New York Times, 21 August 1990

Sheikh Rashid's last official event: Al Maktoum, Mohammed bin Rashid, My Story: 50 Memories from Fifty Years of Service, The Executive Office/Explorer Publishing and Distribution, 2019, p.173; Krane, Jim, City of Gold: Dubai and the Dream of Capitalism, Picador, 2010, p.100

It was subsequently reported: BBC News, 'Sheikh Mohammed Al Maktoum: Who is Dubai's Ruler?', 16 February 2021

The devastating loss: Al Maktoum, Mohammed bin Rashid, My Story: 50 Memories from Fifty Years of Service, The Executive Office/Explorer Publishing and Distribution, 2019, p.175; Krane, Jim, City of Gold: Dubai and the Dream of Capitalism, Picador, 2010, p.100

"What made him happiest during the final days": Al Maktoum, Mohammed bin Rashid, My Story: 50 Memories from Fifty Years of Service, The Executive Office/Explorer Publishing and Distribution, 2019, p.175

Sheikh Zayed would reportedly fly to Dubai: Wilson, Graeme H., Zayed: Man Who Built A Nation, National Archives, 2013, p.519

followed in the next car: Wilson, Graham, Father of Dubai: Sheikh Rashid bin Saeed Al-Maktoum, Media Prima, 1999, p.214

"As Sheikh Rashid was my brother": Wilson, Graeme H., Zayed: Man Who Built A Nation, National Archives, 2013, p.522-523; Wilson, Graeme H., Rashid's Legacy: The Genesis of the Maktoum Family and the History of Dubai, Media Prima, 2006, p.502

"second father": Al Maktoum, Mohammed bin Rashid, My Story: 50 Memories from Fifty Years of Service, The Executive Office/Explorer Publishing and Distribution, 2019, p.78

On February 28, 1991: Chronicle of Progress, edited by Al Abed, Ibrahim, Vine, Paula and Al Jabali, Abdullah, Trident Press, 1996, p.332

Sheikh Zayed would follow on April 24: Chronicle of Progress, edited by Al Abed, Ibrahim, Vine, Paula and Al Jabali, Abdullah, Trident Press, 1996, p.333

CHAPTER 11

"Work is of great importance": 'Zayed bin Sultan Al Nahyan: A Special Tribute,' publisher not identified, 2004, p.22; Gulf News, 'Sheikh Zayed in Quotes,' 31 October 2005

Sheikh Zayed's childhood education: Morris, Claud, The Desert Falcon: The story of H.H. Sheikh Zayed bin Sultan Al Nahiyan, President of the United Arab Emirates, The Outline Series of Books, 1976, p.22

"My philosophy in life is based": Leadership: Collection of Speeches, Stances, Meetings and Instructions of H.H. Sheikh Zayed Bin Sultan Al-Nahyan, President of the United Arab Emirates, 1971-1987, produced and published by Book and Publishing Establishment, documented by Muhammed Khaleel Al-Siksek, edited by Shams Al-Din Al-Doaifi, p.25

often ended his speeches: Sheikh Zayed: Hopes and Deeds, Book and Publishing Establishment, 1990, p.58, p.75, p.88

"When a Ruler becomes conceited and isolates himself": Leadership: Collection of Speeches, Stances, Meetings and Instructions of H.H. Sheikh Zayed Bin Sultan Al-Nahyan, President of the United Arab Emirates, 1971-1987, produced and published by Book and Publishing Establishment, documented by Muhammed Khaleel Al-Siksek, edited by Shams Al-Din Al-Doaifi, p.26, translation edited for clarity

"Nothing in the Koran conflicts with progress": Morris, Claud, The Desert Falcon: The story of H.H. Sheikh Zayed bin Sultan Al Nahiyan, President of the United Arab Emirates, The Outline Series of Books, 1976, p.46, p.84

"Islam in its true essence provides guidance": Morris, Claud, The Desert Falcon: The story of H.H. Sheikh Zayed bin Sultan Al Nahiyan, President of the United Arab Emirates, The Outline Series of Books, 1976, p.86

Muhammad Ali: 'Ali late arriving for book tour in Great Britain,' The Ottawa Citizen, 25 September 1991; 'Ali causes stir,' The Globe and Mail, 25 September 1991

"Man cannot discard his previous life": Tammam, Hamdi, 'Zayed bin Sultan Al-Nahyan: The Leader and the March,' Second Edition, 1983, p.270

"A hunting expedition with falcons": Al Nahyan, Zaid bin Sultan, Falconry as a Sport: Our Arab Heritage, Abu Dhabi, 1976-1396, UAE Ministry of Information and Culture, compiled by Yehya Badr, printed in Great Britain by Westerham Press Ltd, p.8-9

ambition to create a landmark mosque: The Emirates Center for Strategic Studies and Research, 'With United Strength: H.H. Shaikh Zayid Bin Sultan Al Nahyan, The Leader and the Nation,' principally authored by Andrew Wheatcroft, 2004, p.297-298

third largest mosque in the world: The Emirates Center for Strategic Studies and Research, 'With United Strength: H.H. Shaikh Zayid Bin Sultan Al Nahyan, The Leader and the Nation,' principally authored by Andrew Wheatcroft, 2004, p.297

the singer Rihanna: Al Subaihi, Thamer, "Rihanna 'asked to leave' Sheikh Zayed Grand Mosque after photoshoot," The National, 20 October 2013; BBC News, 'Rihanna asked to leave Abu Dhabi mosque over photo shoot,' 22 October 2013

"Islam is a civilising religion that gives mankind dignity": Trident Press in conjunction with UAE Ministry of Information and Culture, United Arab Emirates Yearbook 2005, p.26, (punctuation edited for clarity); also quoted in Wilson, Graeme H., Zayed: Man Who Built A Nation, National Archives, 2013, p.663

"In these times we see around us violent men": Trident Press in conjunction with UAE Ministry of Information and Culture, United Arab Emirates Yearbook 2005, p.26; also quoted in Wilson, Graeme H., Zayed: Man Who Built A Nation, National Archives, 2013, p.663

"People perish, work endures": Leadership: Collection of Speeches, Stances, Meetings and Instructions of H.H. Sheikh Zayed Bin Sultan Al-Nahyan, President of the United Arab Emirates, 1971-1987, produced and published by Book and Publishing Establishment, documented by Muhammed Khaleel Al-Siksek, edited by Shams Al-Din Al-Doaifi, p.30

three hundred thousand flags and five million light bulbs: Nelson, Barry, 'Mideast feels winds of change,' Calgary Herald, 3 August 1991

Travel and return from spinal surgery and new protocol policy: Wilson, Graeme H., Zayed: Man Who Built A Nation, National Archives, 2013, p.609, p.612-615, p.632

kidneys were failing: Wilson, Graeme H., Zayed: Man Who Built A Nation, National Archives, 2013, p.629

Travel to Cleveland Clinic: Trickey, Erick, "A Palace Away From Home," Cleveland Magazine, 1 January 2003

days leading up to his surgery: Trickey, Erick, "A Palace Away From Home," Cleveland Magazine, 1 January 2003; Wilson, Graeme H., Zayed: Man Who Built A Nation, National Archives, 2013, p.655

call from President Bill Clinton: Wilson, Graeme H., Zayed: Man Who Built A Nation, National Archives, 2013, p.655

Movements of Marwan al-Shehhi: United States Government, The 9/11 Commission Report: Final Report of the National Commission on Terrorist Attacks Upon the United States, 2004, p.8, p.224, p.238, p.285

watching live on television and summoned his advisors: Wilson, Graeme H., Zayed: Man Who Built A Nation, National Archives, 2013, p.659

CHAPTER 12
He expressed his condolences to the United States: Wilson, Graeme H., Zayed: Man Who Built A Nation, National Archives, 2013, p.660

around 1,800 arrests: Worth, Robert F., 'Mohamed bin Zayed's Dark Vision of the Middle East's Future,' New York Times, 9 January 2020

"The UAE clearly and unequivocally condemns": Trident Press in conjunction with UAE Ministry of Information and Culture, United Arab Emirates Yearbook 2005, p.27

First Arab country to commit troops in Afghanistan: Saab, Bilal Y., 'In Afghanistan, the Gulf Arab states stepped up,' 1 September 2021, Middle East Institute

"Some citizens wonder": President George W. Bush Remarks on Iraq, Cincinnati, Ohio, 7 October 2002

"If you want to make issue with one of your brothers": Morris, Claud, The Desert Falcon: The story of H.H. Sheikh Zayed bin Sultan Al Nahiyan, President of the United Arab Emirates, The Outline Series of Books, 1976, p.55-56

"It is of course easy to give an answer": Morris, Claud, The Desert Falcon: The story of H.H. Sheikh Zayed bin Sultan Al Nahiyan, President of the United Arab Emirates, The Outline Series of Books, 1976, p.59-60

"Developments move very fast": Sheikh Zayed Letter to Arab League, 1 March 2003, reproduced in Gulf News, 'Zayed urges Saddam to resign, go into exile,' by Dahi Hassan and WAM, 2 March 2003

refused to allow Sheikh Zayed's proposal to be debated: NBC News, 29 October 2005, 'Did Saddam accept exile offer before invasion?'; CNN, 'Arab leaders declare opposition to war in Iraq,' 2 March 2003

"dirty psychological warfare": Shadid, Anthony, 'UAE Urges Hussein To Go Into Exile,' The Washington Post, 2 March 2003

four secret meetings: Fattah, Hassan M., 'Arab League Plan for Hussein Exile Went Sour, Arab Leader Says,' The New York Times, 2 November 2005

"Our last-ditch hope was that Saddam": Bush, George W., Decision Points, Crown Publishers, 2010, p.253

UK Government's own inquiry: BBC News, Chilcot Report: Findings at-a-glance, 6 July 2016

"The Arabs unfortunately didn't have the courage": Shadid, Anthony, 'UAE Urges Hussein To Go Into Exile,' The Washington Post, 2 March 2003

"During those days, the circumstances we worked under": Quote from documentary aired on Al-Arabiya, referenced in NBC News, 'Did Saddam accept exile offer before invasion?,' 29 October 2005

"Homelands are eternal, but presidents and leaders": Gargash, Anwar Mohammed, article in Al Ittihad newspaper, referenced in The Daily Star, 'Mixed verdicts on Sharm el-Sheikh summit,' 4 March 2003

editorial in a major Saudi newspaper: al-Rashed, Abderrahman, editorial in Asharq al-Awsat, referenced in The Daily Star, 'Mixed verdicts on Sharm el-Sheikh summit,' 4 March 2003

Other commentators questioned: The Daily Star, 'Mixed verdicts on Sharm el-Sheikh summit,' 4 March 2003

UAE Government raised it again: Emirates News Agency, 'UAE raises its proposal on Iraq at GCC meeting,' 2 March 2003

more than five hundred thousand lives: Bump, Philip, The Washington Post, '15 years after the Iraq War began, the death toll is still murky,' 20 March 2018,

"I totally agreed with Sheikh Zayed": Emirates News Agency, 'Sheikh Zayed's initiative would have saved Iraq: Arab League Chief,' 28 July 2008

CHAPTER 13

In the immediate aftermath of the September 11 attacks: Worth, Robert F., 'Mohamed bin Zayed's Dark Vision of the Middle East's Future,' New York Times, 9 January 2020

"In every position of responsibility I serve": Emirates News Agency, 'Mohammed bin Zayed - Statement,' 1 December 2003

2003 National Day address: Emirates News Agency, 'Sheikh Zayed highlights UAE achievements in remarkable speech on National Day,' 2 December 2003

"My dear citizens, work for our nation does not cease": Emirates News Agency, 'Sheikh Zayed highlights UAE achievements in remarkable speech on National Day ... 8th ADD,' 2 December 2003, translation edited for clarity

International reaction to Sheikh Zayed's passing: Emirates News Agency, 'World leaders mourn Sheikh Zayed ... 3rd ADD,' 3 November 2004; Emirates News

Agency, 'Amman City Council names a street after the late Sheikh Zayed,' 10 November 2004; Emirates News Agency, '20 new-born Mauritanian babies named after Zayed,' 8 November 2004

"sagacious leader who worked for global peace": Emirates News Agency, 'World leaders mourn Zayed-- 4th add,' 3 November 2004

threw themselves to the ground: BBC News, 'UAE buries father Sheikh Zayed,' 3 November 2004

According to Sheikh Sultan bin Mohammed Al Qasimi: Collins, Laura, 'Life goes on but the grief remains,' The National, 30 November 2011, which references Al Arabiya television documentary

Her Highness Sheikha Fatima receives condolences: Emirates News Agency, 'Fatima receives condolences on Zayed's death,' 7 November 2004; Emirates News Agency, 'Fatima continues to receive condolences,' 7 November 2004

Reactions of world leaders: Emirates News Agency, 'Annan expresses sadness at death of Zayed,' 5 November 2004; Emirates News Agency, 'White House mourns Sheikh Zayed,' 6 November 2004; Emirates News Agency, 'World leaders mourn Sheikh Zayed 15th add,'

4 November 2004; Emirates News Agency, 'Chirac condoles Khalifa,' 3 November 2004; Emirates News Agency, 'World leaders mourn Sheikh Zayed (Queen Elizabeth) 18th add,' 4 November 2004

Interview with Manasir elders: Hoath, Nissar, 'Zayed was a man of many talents, say Bedouin elders,' Gulf News, 8 November 2004; also republished by Emirates News Agency, 'Zayed was a man of many talents, say Bedouin elders,' 8 November 2004

"toughness and daring": Tammam, Hamdi, 'Zayed bin Sultan Al-Nahyan: The Leader and the March,' Second Edition, 1983, p.26

"Death is a natural act": Hoath, Nissar, 'Zayed was a man of many talents, say Bedouin elders,' Gulf News, 8 November 2004, parentheses added [original quote identifies Sheikh Zayed as "Bu Khalifa," which is a term of affection meaning "Father of Khalifa"]; also republished by Emirates News Agency, 'Zayed was a man of many talents, say Bedouin elders,' 8 November 2004

over a thousand mourners per day: Emirates News Agency, 'Thousand line-up to pay tribute to Zayed,' 28 November 2004

a somber and eerie tone: Emirates News Agency, 'Sombre mood envelopes country on National Day,' 3 November 2004

official celebrations had been cancelled: Emirates News Agency, 'UAE calls off National Day celebrations,' 2 December 2004

celebratory lights had not been strung up: Emirates News Agency, 'Sombre mood envelopes country on National Day,' 3 November 2004

"Sheikh Zayed has passed away": Emirates News Agency, 'Sheikh Khalifa Statement/33rd UAE National Day,' 2 December 2004

About the Author

Daniel Slack-Smith is an author and strategic communications advisor with a longstanding interest in the culture and political history of the United Arab Emirates. Originally from Sydney, Australia, he worked in government communications in the UAE from 2007 to 2010. His debut non-fiction book, the authorized oral history *'Killing the Game: The Inside Story Behind the Transformation of Manchester City and the Creation of City Football Group,'* was published internationally in 2018. He lives and works in San Diego, California.

Made in the USA
Columbia, SC
28 April 2024

379da20b-56a2-4d74-9a46-60a0c5393372R01